# Memoir
# of a
# Jaded Woman

# Memoir
# of a
# Jaded Woman

## Tainted Love

# Emunah La-Paz

HSP
Gilbert, Arizona
2487 S Gilbert Rd 106-(283) Gilbert, AZ 85295

Please Contact Ingram Content Group For More Information.

www.ingramcontentgroup.com

This book is not intended as a substitute for the physiological advice of physicians. The reader should regularly consult a physician in matters relating to his/her mental health and particularly with respect to any symptoms that may require diagnosis or medical attention.

From the author: I have tried to re-create events, locales, and conversations from my memories of them. In order to maintain their anonymity, in some instances I have changed the names of individuals and places. I have also changed some identifying characteristics and details such as physical properties, occupations, and places of residence to protect the privacy of the individuals.

The information and views set out in this publication do not necessarily reflect the o fficial opinion of Hubbard Small Press Publications and the author. Neither Hubbard Small Press Publications, the author and bodies, nor any person acting o n their behalf may be held responsible for the use that may be made of the i nformation contained therein.

*For Hope*

*The important work of moving the world forward does not wait to be done by perfect men.* – **George Eliot**

# Contents

# Foreword

To find out that your husband has been cheating is devastating; to find out that he has cheated down, is even more disturbing, for many women.

Judie, a gorgeous model, found out the hard way when she discovered an unflattering picture of a woman whom her husband had been having an affair with.

Judie finally takes matters into her own hands by asking the question every tired victim of infidelity should be asking themselves: "Why?"

Freelance writer Emunah La-Paz took an interest in Judie's story and from there conducted research and interviews surrounding Judie's situation.

The feedback concerning this topic attracted responses from all angles.

This book maintains the point of view of the married man, the so-called unattractive woman, and the jilted, beautiful wife.

## Foreword

If you want to find out why married men cheat—or why some men choose an unfaithful path—this nonfiction, straight-to-the-point volume, gives an honest, viewpoint from both, sides, of the jaded, issue at hand.

# Introduction

It was May of 2011, and I had just settled down to catch up on my weekly gossip. It was something I often felt guilty about doing, yet the stimulating, entertaining lineup of outspoken women masterminded by the queen of inquiring minds herself, Ms. Barbara Walters, started off my day with a shocking story of scandal. And no one can slice the juicy details of factual news events wide open like a ripe melon better than the girls on the daytime TV talk show *The View*. There they sat huddled around the signature table: the feisty redheaded comedian Joy Behar; the vibrant blond candid talk show personality Elisabeth Hasselbeck; and the witty and charismatic talk show host/comedian Sherri Shepherd. The hot topic was moderated by none other than famed Academy Award–winning actress Whoopi Goldberg. I was stunned, to say the least; the timing of the recent scandal could not have been more indicative of the book based off the blog I'd just released in April of 2011, entitled *Why Do Married Men Cheat with Unattractive Women?*

# Introduction

The audience was appalled by a picture of a woman whom society had judged as unattractive. The woman showcased larger than life on the wide screen had sparked a flame of mockery and ridicule, which had now made its way across newsrooms like a blazing inferno. The "unattractive" mistress, now labeled as a home wrecker, was found guilty for having a baby out of wedlock by a well-known married man. A legendary action hero and the former governor of a renowned, populous state, not to mention his lovely, eloquent wife, a striking journalist, bestselling author, and the winner of many influential awards, was now thrust into this scandal, all caused by the husband's lustful desire.

I watched as the audience of *The View* gasped openly in disparagement of the picture of the rather robust fifty-year-old mistress, a shocked clamor so overwhelming that the forthright hostess Whoopi had to reprimand the crowd for their ill behavior, which, in her own words, painted a vision that beauty is in the eye of the beholder.

I worked for ten years as a commercial model. Oftentimes, the worlds of commercial models and runway models would cross paths. I will never forget this one regal model named Judie. A tall, slender, beautiful woman with eye-catching features who had graced the cover of numerous high-end magazines, she was a dream to behold. What made Judie different, though, was that she didn't believe so. Her then husband, a brilliant photographer, had cheated on her more than once, and Judie was devastated. After meeting Judie, I couldn't help but notice that there were so many other gorgeous beauty queens out there who had also been betrayed, yet none of them seemed to carry themselves like Judie during their trials and tribulations. Judie seemed eager to find out why. She wanted to know why her husband, whom she had

# Introduction

planned to build a family with, opted to run into the arms of some other woman, a woman completely opposite in size and physical appearance. Curiosity had captured my thoughts as well, which led me to write this memoir.

# Acknowledgments

A special thanks to all of the women and men who took the time to share their intimate stories.

# Chapter One

I met up with Judie in downtown Phoenix at Houston's, the revered restaurant at the Esplanade on Camelback and Twenty-Fourth Street. Her eyes were red, on account that she had been crying. To be honest, I had nothing in common with Judie—at least that was what I thought at the time. Judie was five foot eleven, extremely slender in build, with thick, flowing blond hair. Not a blemish was to be found on her perfect, chiseled features; her skin was flawless. Meanwhile, I was a five-foot-seven-inch black woman who had to watch my weight continuously to fit the bill as a print model. My skin had mood swings, depending on what I ate; however, my looks were commercial enough to be seen in household ads, billboards, and some industrial films. Nonetheless, deep down inside I envied models like Judie who dominated the industry. Women like Judie, were always off to Milan or London on location; every job they had, it seemed as if they were venturing off onto their next exotic retreat. Me? I was off to the next fast food commercial, trying to make a cold hamburger appear as if it were the best thing I'd ever indulged in. Or better yet, off to meet my commercial husband—who was always much older than I was, might I add—instructed by an overworked photographer to head out in front of a modest house to take a gander at the new, affordable family-sized minivan, with an adjustable picnic table in the back, available at zero interest and with no money down. Big whoop, right? It was boring! I'd often run into some of my fellow model friends who always seemed to clutch a better deal. One of my acquaintances landed a gig as Jennifer Lopez's body double. Now why can't I stumble across jobs like that? I wondered. Now, don't get me wrong; I was happy to get almost anything that came my way. My agent was, and still is, one of the best in the business. She gave her clients what they asked for and made sure all of her models fit the bill and were appropriately groomed in their talent; yet, deep inside, I always wondered how it would be to voyage beyond the sea, getting paid top dollar to wear a sweeping, gorgeous gown. I wanted glamour, and I desired admiration, captured through the eyes of one of the top photographers in the world. To be completely honest, I had been on a few high-profile shoots in which the photographer would ask me to suck in and smile; sometimes, I felt awkward and bloated, this advice did not fare well; either I'd suck in and look miserable, or I'd let it all hang out and look pleasant. As far as I was concerned, there was no in between.

Back then, top modeling opportunities were scarce for African American women in the business. There was Beverly Johnson, the first black model to land on the cover of American Vogue, in August of 1974. Supermodels Iman, and Tyra Banks, did well in the industry. And not to forget, Naomi Campbell, the first black woman to appear on the cover of French Vogue. These women of color, fulfilled the light demand for African American models back in the day. Beauty magazines catering to black women were also scarce. Magazines such as *Ebony*, *Jet*, *Essence*, and *Sophisticate's Black Hair Styles and Care Guide* (in which I was elated to land a spot in their March publication, which featured the beautiful and talented award-winning actress Ms. Halle Berry on the cover, in the early nineties) were a blessing to a female race that at times appeared to be overlooked in a predominantly Barbie-obsessed world. The groundbreaking magazines listed above had a historical presence, eventually capturing the attention of women from all backgrounds and nationalities. In addition, the recognition of the well-respected national publication *Life* magazine, a renowned periodical that presented decades of journalism, often informing and educating our world on the history of African American culture from the times of the civil rights movement to the introduction of the first well-known African American models. On October 17, 1969, *Life* released an issue entitled "Black Models Take Center Stage," featuring veteran model Naomi Sims on the cover. I was not born when this timeless publication was released, yet I was able to obtain a copy from a dear friend of mine who gave me the classic magazine as a gift during my stint in the modeling industry. I now keep the copy framed and hanging in my office, where it serves as inspiration, as well as a visual art piece that encompasses women of color.

Now granted, this motivating accolade did not change my job situation in Phoenix, Arizona; however, it gave me hope that perhaps someday, this odd woman out might receive a winning chance in the spotlight. So, when the opportunity arose for me to finally work for a well-renowned photographer on location in Queen Creek, Arizona, alongside chic models, I was more than ecstatic!

Arriving early to get in for hair and makeup, I was a bit frazzled, to say the least. I was masked in a ton of makeup, so much that I could taste the batter inside my mouth, and the chalky residue made me thirsty, not to mention my head was sore from all the yanking and pulling. I was then escorted onto the set, and once I arrived there, another makeup artist applied even more powder onto my clay-soaked face with an oversized brush. I was buried underneath the bronze powder! I felt like a walking pile of foundation. They had me in a white minidress, and I was so nervous that I was going to get makeup all over the expensive garment.

As I stood fretting, it was then that she appeared. Her name was Judie, and she was also dressed in white, yet her gown was flowing in an angelic form. The difference between us was that, unlike me, this woman was confident in her skin, or so it appeared, until I was instructed to stand next to her; it was then that I could sense a deep sadness. The photographer positioned me on top of a white box because Judie was much taller than I. Judie was a pro! I, on the other hand, needed a lot of guidance, but afterward I felt good about the shoot. Once the session was complete, we went to the back to undress. It was there in the bleak fitting room that the air of confidence that had physically masked Judie's demeanor gradually faded away, leaving behind a desolate canvas upon her face. The woman was now a foreseeable wreck, and her gloom hung over the room like the plague.

I had to ask, "Are you okay?" placing my hand gently on her shoulder as she sat at one of the abandoned makeup stations.

"No. I'm not…he's been cheating on me again." She sniffled.

Handing her a tissue, I asked, "Your boyfriend?"

"No. My husband…I don't know how to let go…" she confided.

"I'm sorry."

She smiled faintly. "All I ever wanted was to be a mother and a good wife. That's what I wanted. I'm so sick of traveling and the lonely nights in hotels. He's never come out to visit me, not even once, since we've been married." As Judie unleashed a flood of tears, thick makeup marked streaks of suntan clay down her cheeks. She looked helpless.

I felt for her. After all, I married a good man who had always looked after my best interests and allowed me to pursue my journey in life. I also had a daughter whom I adored, and at the end of the day, I went home to a family that I loved. Even though Judie lived the perfect fantasy in the eyes of millions of women who were varied in age and lived vicariously through her cover-girl magazine escapades, I realized that at the end of the day, her make-believe world ceased, and reality took place inside a painful, unfaithful marriage.

I was compelled to ask, "Is there anything I can do to help?"

She looked up at me, her deep blue eyes glazed over in deep scarlet shades of red. "Yes, you can be my friend. I need a friend, just…someone to listen to me…that's all."

"Where do you live?" I asked.

"I live in New York. Right now I'm living with an acquaintance in Cave Creek, Arizona. I'm meeting up with my friend at Houston's for dinner. You seem like a nice, caring woman. I don't think in all my years of modeling that I've had one person come up to ask if I was okay. Thank you. Would you like to join my friend and me for dinner tonight?" she asked.

"Sure. I'll have to call my husband to let him know that I'll be home a little late, but it shouldn't be a problem."

"You're married?"

"Yes."

"How long have you been married?" she asked.

"We're going on eight years now."

"Do you have children?"

"Yes." I nodded. "I have a little girl. Her name is Jordan."

Lowering her head, Judie sighed deeply, and then in a faint whisper she disclosed, "I envy you."

———

# Chapter Two

Judie and I sat together, waiting for her friend to arrive at the exclusive spot downtown known as Houston's, nestled across the way from the Ritz Carlton. One of the greatest perks that I enjoyed as a model was the camaraderie shared among fellow models. It was not odd to meet a model on location, then hang out for lunch or dinner afterward. Models stuck together. Sure, some may have their rivals, but for the most part, we all tried to remain peaceful toward one another.

The entire restaurant knew that Judie's friend had entered the venue due to the fact that she was both loud and a bit obnoxious.

"Judie!" she yelled from across the venue as a well-groomed waiter dressed in black escorted her to our booth. "Hi!" She beamed. "My name is Jessie!"

"Hi. My name is Faith." I nodded.

Looking over at Judie, she yelled, "Oh, give me a break! Girl, have you been crying over that scumbag again?" The stout, bleached-blond woman dressed in a revealing tank top then sat beside her heartbroken friend.

"I'll be okay," Judie said as she took a sip of water.

"I'll take a Long Island iced tea, and please don't get stingy with the liquor. I want to be able to taste it, okay?" she told the waitress, and then went on as if she had been there conversing with us for days. "Faith, did Judie tell you that she's been attached to the scum of the earth for over two years now?"

"Jessie, please don't go there." Judie buried her face inside her hands.

"Well, it's the truth!" Jessie rambled on. "I told her that guy was no good. I used to be a makeup artist. I was on location when Judie met that wayward fool. I tried to tell her in the beginning he wasn't no good, but you can't tell a lonely woman anything, you hear?" She pointed toward me. "I tell ya, that man of hers will chase after anything attached to breasts."

"Jessie, please stop!" Judie covered her ears.

"I will not! I am so mad with JT right now, I could just spit fire. Just look at my friend Judie; she's drop-dead gorgeous."

I nodded in agreement.

"What else do you do besides modeling, Faith?" she asked. "You do anything else? Most models in the Phoenix area usually do something else on the side. Work gets a little skimpy every once in a while," she said, not bothering to let me answer the question as she went on jabbering away. "There have been a couple of movies filmed down here, though. I'll be heading off to Tucson to work on a western, and I still do makeup jobs every once in a while. It's something to do, you know."

Just then, the waiter came by with Ms. Jabber Jaw Jessie's drink; she took a long swig as the waitress stood, waiting on her approval.

"Hmm…I've had better." She squinted. "Let's just hope it sneaks up on me later, okay?"

The waitress nodded. Giving us a few more minutes to decide on our order, she left us to the one-way conversation that wouldn't let up on Judie, promoted by Jessie.

"So what did you say you do again on the side?"

"Well, for now I'm raising my daughter, and…I'm actually interested in becoming a writer. I've always been intrigued with women's discussions, so engaging in women's nonfiction is ideal. And perhaps someday even children's books or fables."

"Well, there you go! A writer! I like that! You know what your first book should be about?"

"Ugh…well…"

"I'm glad you asked." She took a long swig of the tonic, and then gasped. "I do believe I can taste the liquor now! Whew! Anyway, I think you should write about men who cheat on their beautiful wives." She patted Judie on the back, but Judie just sat there, broken in spirit. "Yep, that's what you ought to do. The name of the book should be called *Why Do Married Men Cheat with Women Who Look Like Something That Crawled Out of the Sewer?* I can even help you out with your book; I'll write the first chapter on Judie's behalf. I'll be right back—I'm going to find a pad and a pen right now!" she exclaimed, then leapt up.

"Um…actually, why don't you just e-mail it to me? I'll give you my address." I smiled.

"That's an even better idea! I'll do that! I'll be right back," she said as she began hopping from side to side. "That drink went right through me, straight to the ol' bladder. I gotta use the little girls' room. I'll be back—oh, when that waitress returns, put in my order. I want the stuffed pork chops and loaded potatoes." She then ran off, disappearing around the corner.

Judie apologized. "I'm sorry. Jessie is just an acquaintance I met on location while I was on a shoot in Sedona. That's where I met JT as well, and she did try to warn me, but I thought she was crazy." She paused, brushing her fingers through her hair. "And you can see why."

"Well, I do like the idea she had about writing your story; it could even be healing for you."

"No way! Once I get out of this mess, I'm done. I don't want a book about my failed marriage following me around."

I enjoyed my dinner at Houston's. I could have done without Jessie by the time our meal was done; Jabber Jaws was a bit belligerent and drunk. She absolutely had a vendetta against Judie's soon-to-be ex-husband, JT, but I was not sure what it could be about. I was, however, drawn to the idea of writing Judie's story, but her being unwilling to do so at the time would make it very difficult; however, I did end up receiving a letter on Judie's behalf from Jessie. Her e-mail was vicious and rude toward the other woman. Needless to say, if I were to write a book on this sensitive subject, I could not use the verbiage presented in Jessie's original e-mail. Let's just say that I knew sailors who used cleaner language. I had to clean it up, yet sad to say, even when the letter was revised to be suitable enough for a reading audience, some readers were livid!

It was a simple case of "damned if you do, damned if you don't." Yet toward the end, I was soon to discover that Jessie was speaking from her own private pain, which had left a dangerous mark of unforgiveness.

# Chapter Three

I met up with Abella at a quaint little coffee shop in Litchfield Park. Our friendship emerged at a runway gala sponsored by an up-and-coming Latino fashion designer who specialized in wedding gowns, as well as extravagant evening dresses. It was there that Abella, along with two other Latino runway models named Catalina and Gabriela, introduced herself. Ever since then, I considered these women to be my very good friends… well, at least for a brief moment in time. Out of the three, I respected Abella the most; nonetheless, I was intrigued by Gabriela's amazing eye for art, and Catalina…um, let's just say that we tolerated one another. However, I never got tired of hanging out with Abella. She was beautiful, with her thick, black, overflowing hair framing her face like a precious work of art and her soft-brown eyes, passionately seeking understanding, as well as eager to be understood. On this day, I couldn't help noticing that Abella appeared frail and that her eyes looked drained.

"Are you okay, Abella?" I asked as we sat at the umbrella-covered bistro table.

Never beating around the bush, Abella spoke the truth. "No, I'm not, Faith. I'm sick…really sick," she admitted.

"What's wrong?"

Looking off into the distance, she said, "I don't know yet, but I know something is wrong. I went to the doctor's, and they say it may be cancer. I've been so tired lately, and…well, what hurts my heart the most is…Emilio. I found out that he has been cheating on me."

It took a moment to absorb what Abella was telling me. Emilio and Abella had been dating for over five years, and they were engaged to marry next year. Abella had been planning this wedding ever since I could remember. Emilio was the love of her life; that's all she could ever talk about. How could Emilio do such a thing? And now she was sick—and cancer, of all things, could be the cause? She was so young—only twenty-three years old. She had an old soul; not many twenty-three-year-olds are ready to settle down, especially with an okay-looking man like Emilio. Abella could get any man that she wanted, yet she chose a lazy man who was constantly in and out of construction jobs; regardless, I never thought Emilio would cheat on Abella.

"I'm so sorry, Abella." I grasped hold of her feeble hand. Abella was such a noble woman; I could only hope that her suffering would end. "Does Emilio know that you're sick? And that it could be cancer?"

"Yes, he knows, and yet he goes off and cheats on me with this other woman."

"How did you find out?"

"He kept coming home late, smelling like cheap perfume. He smelled nasty, Faith. Finally, I demanded the truth from him, and that's when he told me he'd been seeing someone else."

"Who?"

"I don't know, Faith, and I don't care. I'm just tired of the whole thing. I left him, and I'm living with my mom for now. I'm actually preparing to move to Texas to undergo further testing. I'm going to stay with my aunt. I just wanted to say good-bye, Faith, in person. You've always been a good friend to me."

"You're leaving for Texas? Well…did you tell Catalina and Gabriella?"

"No." She shook her head despairingly.

"We're meeting up tonight at El Zocalo. Maybe it'll do you some good to get out, Abella."

"No. I don't want to be around all that nonsense, Faith. I had the strangest dream about Catalina…" She paused, deep in thought.

"What was it?"

"She was holding a cat, and the crazy animal kept hissing at me, trying to scratch me. It was so bizarre! I don't want to hang out with those girls. I'm done with Catalina and Gabriella; they both need to grow up. It's just the same old drama over and over again." She sighed. "I thought I'd be getting married and buying a house with Emilio; instead, I'm sick and heading out of state."

I felt bad for Abella, and most of all I knew that her dream did not foreshadow good fortune; the cat that she visualized was a warning sign of deceit. I did not try to coax Abella to go out with me that night. Even though I thought that meeting up with the girls could do her some good, I could tell in her eyes that she was done with her modeling sisters for good, and that night would prove to favor a wise choice on her behalf.

When I arrived at El Zocalo, located at the historic Monroe Building in Chandler, Catalina and Gabriella were comfortably seated, indulging in margaritas. As I sat down, I couldn't help noticing that Gabriella was beaming, grinning from ear to ear. Usually, Gabriella was always down in the dumps over her on-again, off-again boyfriend, Fausto, but it was apparent that Gabby had probably received a call from him, and now all was good in her world.

"Let me guess, Gabby: you finally heard from Fausto?"

She smiled. An attractive Latino woman, Gabriella always put me in mind of the sultry entertainer Shakira. She had a flair for designing clothing, and she had dreams of launching her own clothing line someday. Gabby also desired to attend a top-notch fashion-design school in New York.

Be that as it may, Gabriella was a reserved dresser, always sporting a buttoned-up blazer that she never had the courage to remove in public, which was odd, being that she worked off and on as a runway model for upcoming Latino designers in the business. Gabby argued that the clothes she sported on the runway were glamourous, not at all cheap looking like the clothing one would find in some mundane clothing store. She laughed aloud in reference to Fausto. "Yes, I heard from Fausto, and he's meeting me here tonight. I'm going home with him."

She giggled like a schoolgirl, and Catalina echoed her laughter. "Yeah, and we all know who I'm going home with tonight." She winked over at Gabby rather secretively.

"Who?" I asked. "Your husband and five-year-old daughter? The two people you should be going home to?" I intervened.

"Don't start with me, Faith. Just don't start," Catalina said, rolling her eyes as she took a sip of her margarita.

I really tried to understand Catalina, but as time moved on, I came to realize that she had a way of making people feel sorry for her. She thrived off what I called pity-party attention; she used her sad stories to try and justify her selfish desires, or so it seemed. Catalina wasn't bad looking. She had black shoulder-length hair, an infectious smile, and high cheekbones, but her eyes were squinty and cunning, making it hard for me to discern her genuine nature. I can't lie: Catalina got on my nerves, and I was equally aware that I got on her nerves as well.

"I have a new man in my life now, Faith." Catalina, whom we called Cat, smiled cunningly. "He treats me good, not like that deadbeat husband of mine. My new man takes me out all the time; he buys me gifts. I'm meeting up with him after I leave here."

"Cat, you're married to a really nice guy, and you have a daughter, who loves—her father, right?"

"Faith." She shook her head in disgust. "You're just like my mom: you think things are so easy. Just do the right thing, and everything will be okay, right?" She sneered. "It's not that simple. Eduardo is a mama's boy. He worshiped her, and now that she's passed away, all he does is sit there like a big rock. He don't move or nothing; he just sits there and sulks and cries for her. I'm sick of that mess. I need to move on; he's dead weight." Just then, her cell phone went off, and Catalina's eyes lit up as she looked down at the fluorescent screen. "I gotta take this call." Leaping up from the booth, she hustled out onto the patio.

"She's a mess, huh?" Gabby smiled sheepishly. "You know who she's cheating with, don't you?" she asked, taking a sip of the icy margarita and dying to sing—like a canary

"No, who?" I asked eagerly.

"Emilio."

"Huh?"

"You heard me." Gabby shook her head in confirmation of the truth.

"Abella's Emilio?"

"Yeah." Gabby nodded. "Catalina's a skank, but she can't help it —her dad left when she was a kid." Shrugging her shoulders, she peered out onto the patio to make sure Catalina was still out there. "That girl don't have any morals. She's done this before with a married man! She told me all about it. I tried to tell her that it was wrong, but you know that girl is loco." She gestured, making swirling cuckoo signs next to her temple with her index finger. "I think she may have some deep issues. She's so promiscuous."

"Yeah, Cat may have some problems that we don't know about. My heart goes out to her, if she is suffering from some kind of problem that has to do with her dad abandoning her as a child. A lot of women are dealing with dad issues. And because of their unresolved issues concerning their dad, they pick the wrong guy. Still, that's no excuse to go out and cheat on her husband with her best friend's fiancé. Cat should want to do better to spite her hardships."

"I agree, Faith. I told her this, but she's so stubborn. I even tried to get a hold of Abella. I left so many messages, but she won't return my call. Have you heard from her?" Gabby asked.

"Yes, I heard from Abella. She's sick, Gabby, and she knows that Emilio has been cheating. She moved out, and she's living with her mom for now, but she's leaving for Texas to live with her aunt. She's moving there to undergo further treatment...Abella may have cancer."

"Cancer?" Gabby's eyes filled with worry. "That's so awful, Faith."

"I'm done hanging around Cat. I think she's heartless for cheating with Emilio, and I'm going to tell her. You should stop hanging out with her, too, Gabby."

"Faith, I…" She paused for a second. I could tell the drink was going to her head as she struggled to compose herself. "I know, but…I can't."

"What do you mean, you can't? She's nothing but trouble, Gabby!"

"I know she's a hoochie mama. I don't like that about her, but… she can be a good friend. You know we go out a lot!"

"Yeah, so what? Find someone else to hang out with."

"I can't. She's been a faithful friend. One night I was sick. I had way too much to drink, and I threw up in the parking lot. Cat was there for me. She held my hair back while I puked, and then afterward she let me crash at her place."

I gave Gabby a look of disapproval.

"Ugh." Gabby rolled her eyes. "There you go!"

"What?"

"That judgmental look you're giving me right now. I hate that, Faith. Abella used to do the same thing. Cat says that Abella is uppity, just like…" She paused, staring at me with her eyes glazed over in a buzz-like haze, as if she'd said too much.

"Just like what?" I asked.

As she took a sip of her margarita, her eyes told the secret: Cat thought that I was uppity, just like Abella.

"Well," I huffed, "I don't care what Cat thinks, Gabby." I tried to persuade Gabby to rethink her friendship with Catalina. She couldn't be trusted, and I knew this. "You keep talking about how you want to do better in life. It starts with your choices in friends. Cat is deceitful. Abella had a dream that Catalina was holding a cat, and now to find out that Catalina's been cheating with Abella's fiancé…it's wrong. Just look at you." I gestured toward Gabby. "Look at the predicament you're in. You said you were done with Fausto. I don't know what you see in him in the first place. He has you on a string like a puppet, Gabby. He only hangs out with you when he wants to, and you sit there waiting for him like a helpless little puppy. Don't you get tired of his games? He has you on an emotional roller coaster."

"I know. But…I love him, Faith. He's so charismatic, and he can get any girl he wants, and these women," she sighed, "they're so beautiful, gorgeous bodies and all. I just——"

"Gabby, you're just as beautiful as any of those women, and you have a beautiful body. You need to believe in yourself." I tried to encourage my insecure friend. It was strange, she was confident on the runway, but after the show, her confidence seemed to fade away. And she was insecure when it came to love. "Gabby, I don't know what you see in Fausto anyway!" I sighed. "He should change his name to Fatso because he's out of shape."

Gabby laughed. "He used to be a wrestler in high school; he's big boned."

"Yeah, you can do better. I bet if you took your jacket off, a crowd of hopeful single bachelors would flock to you! You don't need Fausto."

Gabby was very well endowed in the chest department—no breast implants; all natural—and shaped like an hourglass. The only time Gabby displayed her belongings was when she was working the runway, featuring a designer dress.

"Seriously? I don't want dudes coming up to me just because of my big breasts. As a matter a fact,"—she smiled, lost in thought

—"there's only one dude I'm interested in, and he already knows what I'm working with." She laughed aloud as she shimmied. "My twins belong to Fausto! I'm thinking about getting his name tattooed across my chest: 'Fausto's Chicas' is what I want scrolled straight across." She laughed boisterously.

"Are you serious?" I asked.

"Come on, Faith, I'm just playing. If I feel good enough, I'll probably take my jacket off tonight. I designed a cute blouse, and I'm dying to show it off!"

"I don't know, I worry about you, Gabby."

"Don't worry about me, Faith. You're too serious, just like Abella. You're going to get sick, too, if you don't calm down. Her sickness is probably caused by stress, and that girl worries about everything—just like you, Faith!"

I sat for a moment, watching as Gabby sipped on her margarita while looking around feverishly for Fausto to arrive. As I waited for Catalina to return so I could rip into her, I was approached by a handsome gentleman, a fine replica of the Latino model William Levy, only with darker hair.

"Would you like to dance?" he asked in his velvety voice. This nice-looking fixture managed to ease my tension instantly.

"Go ahead. I'll watch your purse." Gabby smiled.

I followed the suave gentleman out onto the dance floor. As I attempted to salsa, I faced the sad reality that my body was severely allergic to rhythm. Whoever said that all black people can dance has never run across me on the dance floor. I must have been standing in some other line when God was handing down rhythm, because there was nothing going on from the waist down; nonetheless, my beautiful dance partner tried to encourage me.

"*Vamos! Bailar!* Come on, dance! Move your hips," he kept urging as I tripped over my feet trying to keep up with him. It was a mess; nonetheless, I was having fun.

I must say, I have a love for the Latino culture. I spent the majority of my childhood within the community. In the beginning, I had a hard time adjusting. In my younger years, I was subjected to ridicule at times; however, this quandary followed me among every race, and I came to realize that regardless of culture, the way in which I was treated or mistreated was based on the characteristics of that individual's beliefs. As I got older and more confident in my personal principles, my personality attracted individuals who shared my same passion in life, which at the time was entertainment and fashion. My Latino friends knew how to entertain, and through vibrant colors, they embraced their own sense of style. "Just give a reason, and we'll throw a party" was how they rolled. I loved the festive music and the food: menudo, *macha* beef, tamales—which were highly favored over the Christmas holidays as well—and chorizo with eggs wrapped in a warm tortilla were just a few of my favorite dishes. The warmth of family celebrations was clearly expressed for all to see: birthdays, *quinceañeras*, weddings, graduations—these significant occasions were celebrated within large family gatherings and among close friends with great fondness. Nonetheless, there was drama almost every day; it was like watching a novella or Spanish soap opera—and right now, an unforeseen episode was about to unfold, right in front of my eyes.

As I struggled through the box step on the dance floor, my eyes caught hold of Fausto as he strolled into the room like some kind of celebrity. He greeted his posse at the door, escorted by not one, but two *mamacitas*—a bleached blonde and a brunette—and these women were letting it all hang out. Everything was on display for all to see, no jacket included.

I quickly looked over toward our table and watched as Gabby staggered onto her feet, fiercely making her way over to Fausto; she was livid. Explaining to my dance coordinator that I had to catch up to my friend, I struggled to make my way off the dance floor, but my efforts to reach Gabby came too late. She caught Fausto off guard, and out of her sheer frustration she began pummeling him on top of his bald head. Gabby was also a couple inches taller than Fausto in heels, making her abusive mission effortless as she turned Fausto's round head into a human punching bag. Security finally intervened, restraining the light-weight female boxer in the orange buttoned-up blazer. It was so embarrassing; I didn't know what to do. I knew if I tried to reach out to Gabriela at this time, she would be inconsolable; after all, she'd been drinking as well. So, I did what was best: I grabbed my purse, which Gabby was supposed to be watching, and left for home. Even though I longed to confront Catalina, I know there's a time and a place for everything, and right now was neither the time nor the place.

---

It was Friday evening, and I had just arrived home after having completed an all-day infomercial promoting an amazing energy drink that had the ability to increase workout momentum. Basically, I spent the majority of my day working out practically nonstop, and I was far from energized; all I wanted to do now was go to sleep. A phone call from Judie changed my plans though. I was thrilled to hear from her. She'd been MIA for a couple months and had just flown in for the weekend and was asking to stay with me. Even though it was short notice, her timing couldn't have been more perfect. My husband was in Portland on business, and my daughter was staying over at her grandmother's house for the weekend. Unexpectedly, Judie's arrival brought about new prospects.

She arrived around eight that night, and once again she'd been crying. She wore her anxiety like a depressed porcelain doll. We embraced one another, and I helped her unload her luggage into one of the spare bedrooms.

Looking around, she let out a sigh as if she were unloading the weight of the world from her shoulders. "You have a lovely home, Faith," she said. Walking over to the shelf decorated with family photos, she picked up a picture of me and my daughter, Jordan. We both were newly breaking into the business as a mother-daughter duo back then, so we were all smiles. "She's beautiful." Placing the picture down gently, Judie smiled, deep in thought. "You know, I've been thinking about the opportunity to tell my story, and I want to do it. I'm in so much pain. Every day I think about JT and his betrayal, and I just want to move on, you know?"

"I understand." I nodded. "Why don't you take a load off? I'm sure you're tired." I pointed over toward the coach. "Can I make you some tea?"

"No, I'm fine." Sitting down tentatively, she announced again, this time firmly, "I want to tell my story, Faith. I think it will help others. I know I can't be the only one going through this. You know?"

"Yes, I understand. So what brings you back to Arizona? Where did you go? Are you here on business?" Settling across from her, I was eager to find out what she'd been up to.

"I couldn't stay with Jessie; she was really hounding me about JT. So, I flew back to New York, packed up all of my things back at the condo, then took off to Seattle. My mom lives in Spokane, and I went to stay with her for a while." Nervously, she sucked in her bottom lip, pausing for a second. "He kept calling my mother's house. It was so annoying. I told him that I was thinking about telling my story, and do you know what he said?"

"What?" I leaned in.

"He said he wanted to tell his side as well. Can you believe that? What side of the story could he possibly have to tell? He cheated on me. He's here in Phoenix, you know. He's the photographer on location."

"On location?" I asked. "Are you out here on a photo shoot?"

"Yes. It's up in Sedona again. I'm to report early Monday morning, and then afterward I'm off on location to Trianon Palace, in Versailles, France. I can't believe it: my soon-to-be ex-husband will be on location with me," she said, shaking her head. "He wants to meet up with me tonight at Barcelona in Scottsdale. I told him that I was going to hang out with you, and I referred to you as my biographer. Now he wants to meet you, to tell his side of the story. He's so full of himself, Faith."

"Well, wait a minute." I thought for a second so that I wouldn't sound as tactless as her ex did. "I think he has a point, Judie."

Her forehead wrinkled; she was openly upset. "Are you kidding me?"

"No. Now hear me out, Judie. I think the ability to capture all aspects of your ordeal would shed light on this dilemma. Most men aren't willing to talk about their wrongdoings."

"Do you really think JT is going to admit to any wrongdoing?" She laughed aloud. "He's going to make me out to be the worst wife ever! I can see him now! Blaming everything on my shortcomings. It's not right, Faith. I don't want JT involved."

"Judie, I think we should meet up with him tonight at Barcelona. It's a relaxed atmosphere and all, and I think this is the perfect opportunity to get a male's perspective and get closure for yourself. Don't you want to know his side of the story, Judie? And aren't you just the least bit curious about the other woman? Please don't say no," I cautioned. "We both know you'd only be fooling yourself. You owe it to your conscience to uncover the truth."

Sighing deeply, she said, "I haven't seen him face to face since I left. All of our hate and animosity has been played out over the phone, and I guess it would break the ice since I have to face him on Monday."

"Rationality will get you through this—that and unconditional prayer."

"Hmm…you know, I tried many times to get JT to go to church with me, then he finally went one time—and fell asleep; he obviously missed the sermon on adultery that day." She paused in deep recollection. "You know, Faith, I believe I owe it to myself to find out straight from the horse's mouth. I want to know what made him so unhappy about our marriage that he had to go out and cheat! Yes, I want to hear his excuse.

"I was the perfect wife; at least I tried to be. We had a huge wedding right here in Arizona, close to where we first met up in Sedona…To think it was all for nothing. This was supposed to be my happily ever after. I deserve to know what happened to my marriage," she repeated once again, only this time her sadness had kindled into anger.

———

# Chapter Four

Barcelona was the spot in Scottsdale, Arizona. Women were dressed to the nines, and men dressed to impress. Its grand entrance, decorated with flaming torches, led to an enchanting ballroom known as the Dome. A wine room and the south dining room were the entire rave, and its patio showcased the gigantic, well-lit gazebo. We were able to reserve a secluded area located in the wine room. From there, we were able to view the talented live band. The food wasn't bad either; there was an extensive array of seafood. Both Judie and I were starving, and it didn't take us long to put away shrimp cocktail and flatbread pizza. It was getting late, Judie's ex was nowhere to be seen, and by now, Judie was livid.

"Do you see what I have to put up with, Faith?" Reaching for her cell, she checked her messages. "Not one message from that jerk! He's always late! And of all places, he wanted to meet here, at a nightclub!"

"We'll, it's not just any old nightclub, Judie. I enjoy Barcelona. It's not as if he asked us to meet him at some fast food restaurant or something like that."

"Why are you sticking up for him, Faith?"

"I'm not sticking up for him, Judie. I'm just saying...I'm a married woman with a kid. I don't get out much, so it's nice to be able to throw on my little black dress with matching heels and step out every now then, you know?"

"Well, I'm over the club scene. I would have hoped that JT would've had the common decency to meet up in a quaint environment, like a coffee shop or something. This place is a meat market; every other guy in this room is checking us out like bloodthirsty wolves. Would it have killed JT to meet up with us in a nice, serene atmosphere?"

"Judie, can I ask you a question? And please be honest," I asked with a little hesitation, not wanting to escalate her anger.

"Go ahead." She fixed her confused gaze onto me.

"Are you still in love with your ex?"

She quickly looked away, and I could tell that my question brought about shame. "Of course I'm still in love with my ex, Faith, and I'm frustrated with myself because of it. It's not like I had children by the man or anything, but...that was next. I wanted JT to be the father of my children. But obviously"—she threw her hands up in disgust—"JT docs not feel the same way about me. If he did, he would not have wanted to meet here! This place is one big distraction, and to top it off, he's late!"

No sooner had she stated the painfully obvious than a slender man, short in stature and wearing a black blazer over a white T-shirt, approached the table. He gave Judie an awkward peck on the cheek, and she turned away, folding her arms and pouting like a young child. As if he didn't have a care in the world, he fixed his eyes on me. "You must be Faith," he said, smoothly greeting me with a European kiss from the left and then on to the right side of my cheek. In his suave manner, he made himself comfortable in the seat next to me. Waving down the waiter, he ordered a scotch on the rocks, and then asked me, "Can I buy you a drink, sweetheart?"

"Her name is Faith, JT! Not sweetheart, doll face, honey, or anything else like that. Just Faith!" Judie snapped.

"I'm good on the drinks. Thanks for the offer, JT." I gave an uneasy smile. The place was now packed; however, on our side of the room, you could cut the tension with a knife.

"So my soon-to-be ex-wife tells me that you're a biographer who's interested in writing about our story?"

"I'm actually a freelance writer, and yes, I'm interested in both sides of the story."

Judie began a verbal war. "Well, if you want the truth, you might want to leave his side out of the story because he loves to lie!"

"What is your problem now, Judie?" His smooth exterior was beginning to fade, putting me in mind of the blunt reality television judge Simon Cowell. JT shot Judie a look as if he were growing tired of listening to a tone-deaf contestant.

"What is your problem, Jude? I just got here." He leaned forward, and with me being in the middle, I began feeling a bit warm as the two of them carried on with a combat of words.

"That's right, JT." Judie leaned in as well. Visibly upset, she no longer appeared like a poised model; her face was piercing red. "You just got here! You're always late, JT."

"The shoot ran over, Jude! This happens; you know how this business works."

"Stop calling me Jude!" she yelled. "I know how you work, JT. You could have called! After all, it was you who wanted to meet. You gave the time to arrive here, and then you have the audacity to show up late." She drew in deeply, her hands now gesturing all over the place. "And of all places, you wanted to meet up here at this meat market!"

"You know what, Jude?" Raising his hand with caution, he said, "Oops! I meant Judie!" He chuckled. "Let me tell you something: I could have asked you to meet me at the Saint Regis Grand in Rome, Italy. Or showed up carrying a dozen red long-stemmed roses in one hand and a bottle of the best Pinot in the other, and you"—he pointed—"you would still have found a way to tear me down. You're a hot mess, woman. You need therapy." He winked.

"I'm the hot mess? How dare you! You're four hours late, JT, and you find a way to make yourself look like the victim. Can you believe this, Faith?"

They both turned their attention on me, as if I were expected to choose sides. Saved by the waitress's arrival, my mind scurried for the words that would ease the tension between the two of them, but it was clear that this rift was pretty deep. JT took a long swig of his drink and then slammed it down.

I wasn't a skilled therapist; the only thing I had going on was a Wednesday night Bible study that I hosted at my house for women trying to cope through their marriage—and I still don't know exactly how that group came about. Come to think of it, I wasn't sure how I even got involved in this deal with Judie. I shared that I enjoyed writing, and now I'm the mediator for the War of the Roses. Nonetheless, I approached the situation the best way I knew how: with common logic. I tried to console her over the sensitive issue. "You know, there had to be love between you two in the beginning, I guess..." Desperately, I searched for the right words. "I want to know why your relationship ended.

There must have been something that made you both appreciate one another at one point in your lives. Why couldn't you both build affection on that common ground?"

"He's a cheat. A liar and a sneaky man, Faith! There is no common ground," Judie said, arms stubbornly folded.

"Faith, my soon-to-be ex-wife Jude, or Judie—"

"Wait," I intervened and asked, "JT, why do you refer to Judie as Jude?"

My question made Judie uncomfortable, but JT did not mind at all. "Judie has always been a worrywart. I like the song 'Hey Jude,' by Paul McCartney, so I would sing it to her whenever she was upset about something."

"Oh, how sweet." I looked over at Judie, who was still fuming. "Well, don't you think that's a sweet gesture, Judie? His ability to reach out to you through a beautiful, uplifting song?"

"Yeah, whatever." She pouted.

"Faith, you need to understand something about Judie. She's a beautiful woman on the outside; however, she has mad issues on the inside," he said, tapping his forehead in a thought-provoking manner. "I'm a photographer. I have captured beautiful women on film from all over the world; however, many models that I have dealt with in the past have huge hissy fits, similar to the tantrums of a two-year-old child. I feel that oftentimes celebrities and models like my beautiful soon-to-be ex-wife sitting over there, rarely hear the word *no*. They are constantly given every-thing they desire, making it impossible for any mere man to try and please them." Taking another swig from his tonic, he contin-ued. "Do you know, on one occasion this striking woman sitting next to you threw a hamburger at me? She had her reading glasses on. She looked like a psychotic librarian! She was upset because I had forgotten that she was a vegetarian. This vision of beauty also threatened to poke my eyes out with the pointy end of a chicken skewer."

"Are you kidding me right now?" Judie was infuriated. "How dare you get into that story that you're twisting around into a lie?"

"Judie, please calm down," I cautioned.

"But he's twisting the story, making me seem is if I'm the basket case. I can't stand to be in the same space as this rat! I'm sorry I ever agreed to this meeting. I'm done with this!" Leaping up, she stormed off into the crowd.

As I arose to go after her, JT stopped me. "You're wasting your time. She probably stormed off into her favorite place: the bathroom. Let her cool off for a while; she'll be just fine.

"Look," he went on to say, as if nothing had happened. "Judie is crazy, and I'm glad to be out of the relationship. When I first met her, she had that vulnerable act going on. It appeared as if she needed me. And…I wanted to be needed. But it didn't take long for our marriage to hit a sour note. I was being verbally and mentally abused. I tell you," he said, looking around, "if you weren't here, she would have tried to shank me with a steak knife or something."

"Tell me about the other woman. How did you two meet?"

"I met Lara at a fast food restaurant."

"A fast food restaurant?"

"Yep! I was hungry; I can't do rabbit food. I'm a man, and I need meat. One day I had a taste for a juicy double-decker burger with extra sauce, and when I hit up the restaurant, I met Lara. She helped me with my order and a lot more. Lara made me feel good about myself, and she knew how to cook. All men who have ever dated a model know that the majority of them can't cook, and when they do…well…the attempt alone is grounds for divorce. I believe Judie's unhealthy diet was one of the causes behind her insane mood swings. I seriously believe Judie was hungry all the time because she refused to eat properly.

"Faith, I tried to save my marriage. Judie wanted to write a book about the pitfalls of the modeling world. She felt that this would bring closure with whatever it was she was dealing with. I supported her wishes, and everything was going well. I'm not sure what happened with the book, though; it never panned out, for whatever reason." He waved down the waitress. "Are you sure I can't get you a drink?" he asked.

"I'm fine. Thanks."

After ordering another scotch on the rocks—a double this time—he went on to say, "When I enter a room with Lara, I feel that I'm being acknowledged as well. Even though she isn't considered beautiful according to the standards of this world, she makes me feel beautiful, and in return, I'm able to genuinely love her."

Rubbing his temples, he continued, "Faith, I can't pretend to know why some married men cheat. I never thought I would be in this category, but at the end of the day, a man wants to share his life with a woman that treats him respectfully. Hey, I have a list of male friends who also share my view. These guys know how beautiful women can get, and they can all tell you that beauty is the beast."

"Are you still dating Lara?"

"Yeah."

"Do you think she'd be interested in speaking with me?"

"Lara is a doll, Faith; she'll do anything for me—unlike Judie." He sighed heavily. "Everything has to be a special event, not easygoing at all. To tell you the truth, I can't get out of this marriage fast enough. Beautiful women are nice to look at, but anything else beyond that point is a thorn in your side, gravel in your shoe, a slow-leaking faucet of nag, nag, nag, all day long.

"So do you want to meet with her now?" he asked eagerly.

"Meet with who?"

"Lara, my girlfriend," he replied.

"Lara's here?" I looked around the crowded club as if I could pick her out on a wild hunch.

"Yeah, she's at the bar." He pointed clear across the room. "I asked her to wait for me there. Honestly, she's the reason why I arrived late; she had a special dinner planned, and I stopped over at the apartment to grab a bite and a little extra, if you know what I mean."

"So Judie had every reason to be upset with you being late, don't you think? And on top of that, you lied."

"If I'd told her the truth, she would have gotten angry," he responded nonchalantly.

"But she still got mad because she knew that you were lying."

"Hey…" He raised his hands. "There is nothing that I can do to please Judie. It's time to move on. I can't win when it comes to that controlling woman. Now, do you want to interview Lara or not?"

Of course, I wanted to meet the woman responsible for boldly wrecking Judie's marriage, but I was also nervous; if I ran into Judie while interviewing JT's new girlfriend, sparks would fly for sure. Nonetheless, I took my chances.

I made my way to the bar to find a heavyset woman seated there. Her rear end overlapped the bar stool, and she sat there confidently sipping on a mixed drink. She was dressed in black, and her low-cut tank top revealed a tattoo on her right bosom of a skeleton smoking something, perhaps a cigar or a cigarette. It could have been a joint; the bar was dimly lit, and I didn't want to stare too closely.

"Lara, this is Faith, the woman that's writing my autobiography," he boasted. "Faith, this is Lara."

I nodded, then quickly addressed JT's comment. "Actually, JT, the book is not about your life; it's about you, JT." I looked at Lara, then back at JT; both of them looked relaxed, as if nothing really bothered them. I wondered if they'd been smoking the same thing that the skeleton on Lara's right breast had been smoking.

"Look, I see a couple people that I know. I'm going to go say hi and let you two girls talk." Caressing my back, which made me cringe, JT moved over to Lara, giving her an awkward extended kiss upon her pierced lips before making his way off through the crowd.

Looking around to make sure there were no signs of Judie nearby, I sat on the barstool next to Lara. Giving her a look-over once more, I didn't see any blemishes; however, the lights were low. She had a couple piercings on her nose and lips that were a bit distracting, yet I wouldn't haul off and call the woman a sight for sore eyes. To me, Lara appeared lost; a young woman searching, just like any other woman.

"So, is your book about trashing the mistress?" she asked.

"No. I want all angles; that's why I would like to interview you."

"Well, what do you want to know?"

"I know that you two met at a fast food restaurant, but I guess I would like to get to the core of the matter. What caused you to break up a marriage?"

"Trust me, Faith, if it was so happy, I wouldn't have been able to break it up. No woman can break up a union that's solid. JT's marriage had so many unresolved issues. If I hadn't come along, it would have been some other woman, trust me!"

"Don't you care about the simple fact that what goes around comes around?"

"No. Why should I? I hate to sound coldhearted, but every time I hang around JT's friends, the ones that know Judie remind me constantly of how beautiful she is and how repulsive I look. I mean…" She paused, taking a sip from her glass. "They don't just come on out and say it, but by the looks on their faces, I can tell that's what they're thinking. So I decided to bask in the glow! Yep! I'm the big heifer that stole Judie's man! So what? Let the poor little eye candy go out and find herself another guy, preferably some rich dude. Hey, maybe she can become a trophy wife or some mess like that. Would this be much of a story if I were a beautiful model?" she asked, giving an abandoned glare.

"Do you think you're beautiful, Lara?" I asked.

"No, I don't. My mother and my stepfather embedded that into my head early on. But JT thinks I'm beautiful, and he's a photographer. JT gets paid to capture beauty on film, so maybe he sees something in me that I can't seem to find in myself. I need a man like that in my life. Judie can go find herself another man. JT belongs to me now." She smiled with grit. "I don't ask for much. I give the man what he needs when he needs it. In the end, Judie's looks weren't enough to keep her man."

I'd heard enough. I gave Lara my e-mail address to send me her story in writing just in case I failed to capture the nature of her being from memory. It was obvious to me that Lara was dealing with her own pain, and distress often seeks revenge without moral consciousness.

Before leaving, I also gave my e-mail address to JT. He was going to e-mail me his side of the story as well, just as Jessie had. He even opted to have some of his male friends e-mail me information concerning their bad experiences dealing with beautiful women. I was concerned, not wanting to write a book that would cause a witch hunt against attractive women. I wanted to provide views from each standpoint, and by interviewing JT's new girlfriend, I was able to uncover insight from every angle. But I would soon find out that Judie was now no longer interested in telling her side of the story, for fear that everyone would gang up on her.

That night, I found Judie huddled in the extravagant lounge area in the bathroom. The attendant was trying to console her again; she'd been crying. I wanted to tell Judie that I'd spoken to JT's new girlfriend, but there was no way I could muster up the strength to share that information; the woman was in horrible shape.

When we arrived back at my place, Judie told me that she received a call from Jessie, who wanted to meet up with the both of us at Ah-So teppanyaki restaurant, in which a master chef prepares the meal right before your eyes. Jessie wanted to treat us and a group of her beautiful girlfriends who had also been betrayed in their relationships. Judie wanted nothing to do with Jessie and her group of friends, but I talked her into it; I honestly felt that she needed to be around women who were going through the same predicament. What good would hanging around a happily married woman with a kid do for her heart? At times I felt that being around me caused her even more pain. All things considered, I spoke to my husband and daughter frequently throughout the day. Even while we were waiting for JT to show up, most of my time was spent enjoying my husband's company via text. I tried to remain alert toward Judie, who had admirers steadily approaching our table that night. Judie was not interested in other men; she was still hooked on JT. I was worried for her; I could sense that she wanted JT back, in spite of his infidelities. However, one thing remained crystal clear: JT had moved on. There was a new queen in his life, Ms. Burger Queen. Judie was now an outcast vegetarian, tossed to the side like a bag of soggy lettuce.

———

# Chapter Five

I wasn't up for an invigorating jog the following morning; after all, I was still extremely sore due to that crazy infomercial. Yet I went out on a morning jog with Judie anyway, which ended up being a brisk morning walk as she went on to vent about JT's shortcomings.

"It was a mistake meeting up with JT," she shared. "I regret it even more now that I have to shoot with him on Monday. I'm dreading that job! I can't believe he brought up that hamburger incident, completely leaving out the reason why I threw that burger at him in the first place! Faith, I don't go around town just hurling burgers at men, you know?"

"Well, you don't seem like the burger-hurling type." I smiled as we made our way over to a nearby bench shaded by a sprawling oak tree.

"The more I think about it, the more I realize…I'm still in love with my ex, Faith—yet he makes me so…angry!" Balling her hands up into fists, she let out a scream. "Ugh! Why can't I let go of my cheating husband?" Shaking her head in frustration, she continued, "Yes! I threw a hamburger at my ex. Yep, I did it on the night of my birthday. He didn't come home until one a.m. He handed me a hamburger and refused to tell me where he was. I was upset. It was obvious that he was out there having a burger with that other woman when he should have been home with me. He kept coming home late—not to mention the smell! He had a strange odor within his clothing, similar to the smell of canned meat. It was disgusting! I found it extremely difficult to have sex with someone who smelled like…Spam. And in regards to the chicken skewer…" She laughed aloud in sheer annoyance. "That simply never happened. I don't eat meat! Why would I walk around with a chicken skewer?"

Placing her bitter rant on hold, she confided in grief, "It never used to be this way, Faith. When I first met Jonathan, he was everything I wanted in a man: attentive, caring. Jonathan had the ability to capture my physical being with his camera lenses, and his personality captured my heart. Our wedding was right out of a storybook! We got married in Sedona, the Chapel of the Holy Cross. A landmark church embedded in red-rock mountains. It was a beautiful event, one of the best days of my life. And now we're ending our marriage. This may be the last shoot we have together." She began crying. "I love him, but I can't tolerate him! What kind of sense does that make?" She laughed, tears streaming down her face.

I had to ask the question when all other answers for harmony seemed to fail. "Judie, have you tried prayer?"

"Prayer?" She smiled. "Yes, I've prayed for my husband to change, but he won't."

I laughed inside. That's the first thing most women do, pray for their spouse; little do they know that their spouse is praying for them as well—and none of the prayers get answered due to the fact that most couples pray with the wrong motive in mind.

"Judie, prayer isn't witchcraft. You don't pray to have something done in your favor. Prayer can be used to help you get through a difficult time in your life as well. Ask God to grant you the serenity, the wisdom for how to move forward without looking back."

Judie thought for a moment. "I used to go to church with my grandmother. She was a woman of great faith. When she passed away, I stopped attending—and I stopped praying."

"Why?"

"Because…" She paused, seemingly ashamed of what she was about to reveal. "Because God wasn't listening to my prayers. It wasn't working! Maybe I just have a lack of faith."

"Well, you're going to have to work on that, Judie, because it is written that if you have faith as small as a mustard seed, you can move mountains. Pray continually," I shared. "I was watching my husband teach Jordan how to ride her bike. Jordan fell numerous times, but through consistency she was able to get the hang of it. You may not get what you want when you ask, but there will come a day when you will thank God that he didn't give you what you prayed for. Pray for wisdom every day of your life."

Drawing in a deep sigh, she said, "I'll try."

Studying the discontentment in her eyes, I could tell she wanted what every woman desired: companionship.

I could only hope that our outing with Jessie would lift her spirits, because my support alone was not going to help. It would take a village of comfort to help Judie through her torment.

# Chapter Six

"Over here!"

Jessie's rowdy voice carried over the mingling clientele as we entered the restaurant. Sake bombers awaited us as she and a group of women ranging from all backgrounds sat around the teppanyaki table where the entertaining chef wowed everyone with his skills as a culinary master. He sharpened his knives as he waited for his remaining guests to be seated, and of course Jessie took over the room through her forward conversation.

"Listen up! May I have your attention, please!" she yelled. I wondered how many bombers she'd had; Jessie was quite self-assured, to say the least. "Girls! I would like you to meet my beautiful, gorgeous friend Judie! I was her makeup artist on several top-model shoots here in the valley. My friend Ju…Ju… Judie," she stammered, "is a woman! And she is gorgeous, inside…and out! And can you believe that her husband cheated on her? With a big…heifer of a woman?"

I looked over at Judie, who appeared mortified as women on both sides of the table gasped in pity.

Jessie continued. "But she's gonna get back at that good-for-nothing, backstabbing, two-timing, lying scumbag! We all are! We're writing a book, thanks to Faith over there!" She pointed at me. The table of women looked over at me, giving a nod of approval, and then applauded. "Faith is a commercial model who writes on the side! So all of you women who have been jilted and lied to by your good-for-nothing husbands or fiancés or boyfriends, Faith is the woman to talk to! Let's all drink to Faith!"

All the women except for Judie and me lifted tiny teacup sake bombers into the air, then one by one they each proceeded in a rowdy manner to place the shot-like teacup on top of two chop-sticks that rested on top of a shot glass of beer. They pounded their fists on the table, paused, dropping the shot into the beer, and then drank quickly. Consuming the tonic almost in unison, some of the women wheezed afterward, while others grabbed for glasses of water.

I was uneasy. I told Jessie that I like to write as a hobby—now all of a sudden I'm Dear Abby. I didn't like where this was going; I was extremely uncomfortable, to say the least. Tremendously uncomfortable!

After the iron chef had completed his talented showcase, which involved slicing and dicing veggies and flipping shrimp tails into the air and catching them in his pocket, we all conversed over a tantalizing dinner. After we indulged, scattered conversation at the table turned into a women's forum, and the topic at hand was inevitable, initiated by a seemingly timid woman from India; her name was Sushanti.

"How long have you been writing?" she asked.

A bit ill at ease with the question, knowing that in truth, I'd toyed with the idea of writing but never really embarked upon the notion, I wasn't sure how to answer. I just remained as truthful as one could be under this peculiar circumstance.

"I'm a student when it comes to the principles of writing at this point, but I've always had a heart for the worry that we as women seem to face almost on a daily basis."

"Oh, yes!" She smiled shyly. Her voice was almost in a whisper, and I had to listen carefully, tuning out all the other noise in order to sift out her insight.

"Most men don't seem to stress over the minor details that we do. I'm an avid reader, and I can't wait till your book is complete, especially since it touches on a subject that I've endured numerous times. What will you call your book?"

Jessie, who seemed to have no trouble at all hearing anyone, brought the conversation up to hearing capacity so the entire table could join in, even the table next to us if they so wished.

"Sushanti just asked about the title of the book that Faith will be writing on our behalf! We've decided to call it *Why Do Married Men Cheat with Women Who Look Like Something that Has Dropped Out of the Pit of a Donkey's Ass?*"

A faint rush of laughter drifted around the table. Once again, Jessie knew just the buttons to push to make me feel uncomfortable. I now knew that Jessie had the kind of personality that I would simply have to speak out against quickly in order to get my point across.

"Jessie, that's not the title. It's too long, for starters, and offensive. I'm still working on the title."

"I don't think it's offensive at all!" she barked. "We are losing our men, and the women these low-life jerks are cheating with look like something stuck on the bottom of my shoe. They're fat and ugly! Unattractive is what they are."

"Hold it, Jessie!" yelled an attractive, voluptuous woman dressed in red, with an olive complexion and big hair right out of the movie *Hairspray*. "Why does she have to be fat? Why does society define overweight women as being unattractive?" she asked, looking around the table for answers. No one said anything. "I'm considered overweight for my height, yet I bet I can outdance and outperform any one of you skinny heifers. I hate that women with curves are written off as ugly."

Jessie spoke up. "Of course we're not talking about women like you, Boston. You've got Marilyn Monroe curves, and you got class, honey! You are right! There are some beautiful full-figured women out there. I was just on location, doing hair and makeup for some amazing plus-sized models. What I'm talking about is the woman Judie's husband cheated with. You should have seen this girl: bad skin and all, and ugh…the guy must have been plastered when he hit that."

Sushanti spoke up. "Well, the woman my husband cheated with was pretty. At least, I thought she was; however, her behavior was unattractive. She kept hounding me, even at my place of work, throwing my husband's infidelity in my face. Every opportunity that she had was spent on humiliating me until I finally couldn't take it anymore. My marriage was too crowded, so I stepped aside. This woman was beautiful, and she knew what she wanted, which happened to be my husband." Sushanti lowered her head. I could only hope she was not about to cry. Judie had drowned me in her tears, and I couldn't bear yet another crying fest. Yet Sushanti continued, "One day, she showed up while my ex-husband and I were having dinner. There she stood on my doorstep; she kept yelling for my husband to come with her. I asked him, 'Is this what you want? Do you want to leave like this?

44

Do you want to make a mockery of our wedding vows?' He couldn't look me in the eyes. He grabbed up his things and left with her."

"Oh, heck naw!" a loud voice echoed from across the table. Her name was Lameka. "I would've tore that hoe up! Ain't no way some hood rat would show up on my doorstep, talking about, 'Are you ready to go?' I'd be like, 'Are you ready to die, right here, right now, hoe?' That's what I would have told her!" she huffed. "You know what, Sushanti" Lameka pointed toward her. "You one of them soft women who get walked all over. You gotta have a backbone, chile!"

"Lameka, your husband left you, too, for another woman, and I've seen Lamar's new wife; she's not as pretty as you, but she's not unattractive."

Taking another look at Lameka, I saw that she wasn't bad looking at all. She had a nice build and looked as if she worked out. She was well toned and whatnot, rocking a signature Halle Berry hairdo and all; not a bad-looking dark-skinned woman. The only thing that I would deem unattractive about Lameka was her mouth; she was awfully loud, to say the least, just like Jessie.

"I ain't talking about the way that wench looked," she went on to say. "Lamar left me for a rusty, dusty hood rat! She was nasty! The woman had five kids! Can you believe that?" She looked around the table in shock. "Five kids. Now what kind of man is gonna leave his wife with no kids for a woman with five crumb snatchers?" The table pondered for a moment. "He's a whack job!" she yelled out. "That's what he is. And I wish that trash would've came up on my doorstep like that hussy did in your case, Sushanti" She paused. "At the end of that conversation, that tramp would have been hauled off in a body bag!" She nodded. "And if you ask me, the tramp Lamar left me for, that woman didn't look like nothing. She was shaped like a dang U-Haul truck." She poured herself another shot.

Sushanti voiced, "Violence is not the answer, Lameka. The word 'unattractive' can cover so many descriptions, not just the physical. One's behavior can be unfitting as well. I hope your book won't be a mockery of one's physical appearance. My grandmother used to say that no woman has control over how she looks, but evert woman can at least carry herself with a sense of respect." She gave a timid grin before asking her next question of concern regarding this unorthodox book. "Have you obtained feedback from women other than this group of women?"

I thought for moment. I hosted a Wednesday night Bible study at my house, but those women were just as weird as these women. I sat there baffled, in thought.

"Not to be rude, but…" Sushanti peered around the table, making sure that no one was looking in our direction before she continued. "You really should find other women who are wise in their journey concerning this matter. Don't get me wrong," Sushanti cautioned, "Jessie and these women are kind, and they mean well, yet they are undeveloped in the way that they view such a delicate subject. They all seem to focus on the physical nature of infidelity. There should be views from seasoned women who have overcome every aspect of a challenging marriage, whether they were able to hold their union together or not. Your book should go beyond the concept of physical conceptions and touch on all subjects that can cause hardship in a marriage. Infidelity may be a major reason why some marriages struggle, but there are other hardships as well. . You must provide real stories from authentic women that provide wisdom to your readers."

I knew Sushanti was right, but where would I find a seasoned group of women? I considered myself to be young, and naïve back then, as well Sushanti advice seemed challenging at the time, as I had no clue where to find such women. And just when I thought that Sushanti could not possible come up with any more suggestions for the premature book, she asked yet another question.

"And not to be problematic, but does your book have creditable viewpoints from a reliable source? Such as a strong spokeswoman who is familiar with the subject of infidelity due to personal insight?"

"Ugh…No, not at this time. I'm in the early stages, mind you." I was now feeling a bit overwhelmed concerning the mere thought of writing a book.

I knew that this book could not focus on the physical. Beauty fades; our essence should reflect our character, not our carnal appearance. Having a heart for scripture, I knew all too well that "man looks on the outward appearance, but the Lord looks on the heart" (1 Sam. 16:7).

To those who understand scripture, this verse is a beautiful song to the heart; yet to others caught up in a world that chases after physical beauty, this verse is a bitter pill to swallow.

Sushanti's concerns resonated with me. I needed to find a group of mature women who had overcome the obstacle of infidelity and other problems, beyond the matter of infidelity, that challenge the union of marriage. I also needed to find a solid spokesperson who had insight on infidelity due to their own personal journey. I had no idea where I was going to find such women, but eventually, through patience marked by faith, I saw the door leading to such treasure reveal itself.

# Chapter Seven

Judie's marriage had fallen apart, but her modeling career, was on fire. She had signed a lucrative deal with a well-known makeup corporation. Judie was now featured in countless ads, and traveling around the world. Yet I knew that Judie would give it all up to fix her marriage, if she could.

As for me, I was on the lookout for seasoned women to add to my half-baked book. All I had so far was a bunch of women mourning over the deaths of their marriages. I needed experienced women who had weathered the storm. And then one day, my search came to end. Thanks to a good friend at the time, I was introduced to a group of women who were unafraid to share their amazing, heartfelt stories. All of the women attended a Thursday morning women's gathering at a nearby church.

One evening, I invited the women over for dinner and conversation.

This group of seasoned women had dealt with pain on different levels, involving infidelity, family crises, and personal loss. The things some of these women went through may have destroyed the average woman. Each woman dealt with her pain according to her personal strength.

There was Paula, a kindhearted soul; Laura, who stood patiently in her convictions; Sherry, who spoke through grace and humility; Martha, who understood the quality of gentleness through the power of peace; Natasha, who learned to embrace patience in the midst of unforeseen circumstances. There was Rose, in search of the perfect union. And last, there was Natalia, who stood by her faith through an expectant heart.

Seasoned in adversity, these women had experienced life and had words of wisdom to help elevate other women in need of guidance. Their stories were woven together like a tapestry of strength inside my heart.

---

When Paula was married to her husband, Stephen, she dwelled in the mind-set of patience throughout the unsettling relationship.

Despite the fact that Stephen did not provide the compassion that Paula needed to feel appreciated in her role as wife and mother, Paula continued to diligently raise their children in hopes of setting a positive example. Yearning to elevate the action of perseverance during heartbreaking circumstances, Paula fought to be a good mother out of respect for her children. However, over time, Paula's kindness was tested over and over by her husband's abusive behavior, until she finally reached the point of sheer exhaustion.

Inevitably, Paula realized that her one-way relationship did not reflect the kind of empathy that she had wished for in return.

After spending years in an unhappy marriage, Paula realized that her kindness toward her husband was mistaken for weakness.

Most important, Paula recognized that she had spent years invested in a harmful relationship to avoid her fear of loneliness. Eventually, Paula became aware that her peace of mind was what mattered most.

Paula made a bold move by freeing herself from the chains of fear and divorced her husband.

Starting over turned out to be a liberating action in which her new companion is peace enriched with consideration. Paula now knows the true meaning of joy.

Paula's advice: *Don't be afraid to leave a relationship that does not honor you in return.*

Most women like to be in control of their lives, but even self-reliance has a price, as Laura shared.

Laura, a striking woman with classic Marilyn Monroe good looks, was used to being in control. Laura's family provided her with a sense of comfort and protection. Yet once Laura stepped out of her parents' comfort zone to experience life on her own, she realized that not all relationships were safe and reliable.

Laura met her first husband in a clothing store. He was a striking and charming young man. It did not take long for Laura to embrace the gentleman who filled her mind with dreams of traveling to Paris and living a life of romance and adventure. The two were married within a matter of months; the convincing young man who had gained Laura's trust had won her over. As time moved on, Laura realized that her new spouse was full of lies and deceit. The trip to Paris and the romantic getaways were all a con in order to get Laura to marry him. Laura had been deceived. Yet she had taken vows to love her husband for better or worse, so she tried to make it work.

Years passed, and Laura was now stuck in a marriage tainted with verbal abuse and mind games. What concerned her the most were her two young children; she did not want them to suffer in a world of dysfunction. Laura's marriage was falling apart; her husband relied on alcohol. Partying and drinking became the norm for him, and Laura became concerned about his safety. Yet her husband's response was always arrogant when she would express her worries. He would respond, "No one loves me better than me." Laura's concerns finally took root as her husband was involved in a nearly fatal car accident. Her husband had lost control of his car after a night of drinking; the crash caused the sunroof of the car to cave in. Particles from the glass destroyed his optic nerve, making him blind and now dependent on his wife for support. Yet a life sentence of blindness did not diffuse his pride. Laura's husband became even more abusive. Laura and her children spent some nights in a shelter for battered women. Eventually, the abuse became too much to bear, as Laura's husband physically attacked her as she slept one night. Laura survived the traumatic experience, which gave her the strength she needed to leave the deceptive relationship.

Five years had passed, and Laura was now a single mother trying to make ends meet. Laura spent a great deal of her time taking college classes in psychology, making it easier for her to spot a dysfunctional person a mile away. In time, Laura finally agreed to go on a blind date at a well-known bar. Laura's classes came in handy as she instantly picked up on unstable signs in her potential date. Not taking any chances, she quickly moved away from the dysfunctional man by making her way to the other side of the bar. It was there that Laura met a genuine man who asked if he could sit next to her. Of course, Laura studied the man up and down before she allowed him to join her. That night Laura met a mate who was kind in spirit. The two married, and now Laura is living the happy life she had hoped for. Laura often says, "Choose your relationships wisely."

Laura's advice: *If a crazy guy approaches you inside a bar, run to the other side of the room.*

---

"Till death do us part" does not have to be a life sentence, not according to a stunning woman named Sherry, whose piercing blue eyes were reminiscent of those of legendary film star Bette Davis.

Sherry met her husband, Barry, at the American Legion bar in Chicago.

Sherry was not interested in her husband-to-be at the time. Barry seemed to have issues that Sherry could sense a mile away.

But Barry's determination to build a relationship with Sherry became a reality. The two were married, and eventually, they started a family.

The marriage was not what Sherry had envisioned, and she was not living the life she had imagined for herself. In her mind, she and Barry were not meant to be.

Barry had a drinking problem that dominated the relationship to the point that Sherry had to pack up the kids and leave, as she feared for their safety.

Sherry was faithful during this time in her life. She worked three jobs to support her children. Through dedication, Sherry was able to raise her children, and through humility, she was able to build a friendship with her estranged husband up until his death.

By the grace of humility, Sherry was able to clothe herself with compassion for a man who had seemingly given up on himself. Humility can go a long way.

Sherry's advice: *Have compassion for yourself, and take charge of your own life through faith.*

---

To praise in the midst of sorrow, is a hard concept to understand, during a dark- period, that would have destroyed, most women. Martha knows that there are angels on earth who comfort those who are broken in spirit, for a lifetime.

Martha, a glowing and energetic soul, grew up in a small town enriched in strong moral values. Her conservative lifestyle forced Martha to dress modestly during an era of miniskirts and go-go boots.

There came a time when her built-up tension from within longed for independence, and Martha was more than ready to break free from the small town where she was raised.

Martha chased after this desire, which led her into a relationship with a handsome man whom she referred to as DDGM—Drop-Dead Gorgeous Man.

The good-looking gent swept Martha off her feet and into a whirlwind marriage that was not meant to last.

Martha's man had an unfaithful streak that eventually drove her to the point of considering turning her rooster into a hen.

Martha divorced her untrustworthy husband and eventually married again.

Her next relationship was abusive and self-destructive. The only good that came out of it was the birth of her precious daughter.

Martha cherished the birth of her daughter and watched as she grew into a beautiful and loving young girl. Tragically, the lives of Martha's young daughter and a family friend ended abruptly through a fatal shooting initiated by Martha's estranged husband.

Although this event would traumatize many mothers, Martha says that even though her daughter has passed on to heaven, her gentle spirit and sweet essence is felt strongly throughout life here on earth.

Martha has learned how to stay strong through the remarkable gift of serenity.

Martha's advice: *Praise in the midst of sorrow: "You turned my wailing into dancing; you removed my sackcloth and clothed me with joy" (Ps. 30:11).*

My dear friend Rose, a free spirit who flew by the seat of her pants, traveled the world and lived her life vivaciously. Blessed with a good upbringing, the all-American midwestern beauty seemed to have it all. Yet when it came to relationships, she was not convinced that she had found her soul mate.

Married twice, Rose tried everything from church to counseling to mend the relationships. However, those circumstances were not meant to be.

Rose did not end her marriages in hate or regret, and she still remains good friends with the men of her past.

Rose now found herself in a complex relationship, in which she believed that the man she cared for suffered from narcissistic personality disorder (NPD), defined by most clinics as "a cerebral illness in which people develop magnified intellect of their own significance and a hidden need for approval."

Those who deal with NPD can be arrogant, having little regard for the feelings of others. Yet behind this mask of egotism is an insubstantial self-image, threatened by the smallest amount of disapproval." Under these conditions, the perfect marriage seemed out of reach, lost within the depth of adversity. That being said, Rose was brave enough to admit that she too had faults that hindered their relationship, through which she was now aware that there are so many mental conditions that couples are buried under. Many men and women are damaged due to their abusive childhoods. The world's answer to such impairment is prescription drugs to help bury their emotions. Harmful addictions, such as alcohol abuse, help mask the pain.

However, Rose was painfully aware that a false sense of healing without dealing with the spirit leads to a slow death of the being.

Rose's advice: *Seek a higher being with all of your heart. Do not rest on your own understanding. In all of your power, acknowledge your faith, and everlasting peace will see you through.*

---

Last but not least, there was Natalia, a woman who longed to find the right mate. She was a beautiful blond socialite who enjoyed nineties hip hop, relaxing trips, and playful banter among good friends. As time moved on, Natalia had hoped for a lasting relationship.

It seemed as if the world had plenty of outlets for hooking up singles, everything from speed dating to online matchmaking. Yet Natalia was looking for a mate who shared her core faith values. Natalia would have never guessed that her mate would be a man of a different nationality, celebrating different traditions. What mattered the most was that they both shared the same faith-driven principles.

Their meeting was spontaneous, an unforeseen hookup master-minded through faith. The two encountered one another at a once-in-a-lifetime event, an occasion that they never attended again after they met.

Natalia's advice: *God knows the desire of our hearts. Trust his timing.*

---

The women who shared their stories with me would go on to be lifelong friends. And within this special group of women, I was able to find a convicted spokeswoman named Kim Corder, a woman who was unafraid to voice her personal struggle against infidelity. I have saved Mrs. Corder's testimony for toward the end because it deals with a counterintuitive subject that is difficult for women and men to face. Nonetheless, Corder's authentication is one of the key necessities that provide a freeing power against the burden of infidelity.

---

"Can you believe he did that, Faith?" Judie screamed. Even though she was now ocean-covered miles away on location in Paris, she sounded as if she were standing right there in my front room, bawling, ranting, and, raving.

"He brought that woman onto the shoot with him!"

"He did what?" I asked.

"He brought that woman on my shoot. I felt so ashamed."

"Why should you feel ashamed?"

"That's what I keep asking myself. JT was the one who cheated on me, so why am I the one hurting? It's not fair, Faith."

"I know. Just calm down; don't get so worked up, Judie."

"I'm so sick of everyone telling me to calm down! I'm sick of it! I feel so lonely and lost, Faith. I'm in a different country. I don't speak the language. I have no one to console me. Not even my own mother understands. I'm lonely. And yet my ex, he has someone! What kind of cruel fate is this? What did I do to deserve to be treated this way?"

"Judie, I wish I could be there with you."

And this was the truth. I wish I could've been there for Judie, but I was getting Jordan ready for her ballet class, and afterward I was off to Portland to visit my husband. I had a life filled with people who cared for me and respected me, and here I was trying to comfort a woman who was lonely, wishing for stability and genuine love—and for once, I, a person who lived vicariously through the desire of a beautiful fashion model like Judie, wanted nothing to do with her empty predicament.

Yet, I tried to grasp something good out of her painful circumstance.

"Look, Judie…are you there?"

Just as I was about to tell her not to lose heart and that Paris is a place of love or the city of something along those lines, I suddenly felt guilty for not telling Judie that I'd met JT's new girlfriend. Perhaps if I had told her, she wouldn't have been so crushed. I was so frustrated at this point due to the neediness of motherhood; my daughter, Jordan, now had to use the bathroom, which sucked, because I had just struggled to put those darn tights on her, and that snug-fitting, fluffy, pink, stupid ballet tutu. They really ought to put snaps on those things for little girls with weak bladders! Ugh! Now I had to take the stupid thing off so she could use the stinking bathroom! And just as I struggled to do so, now someone was clicking in on the other line; most likely, it was my husband calling to go over my itinerary. I wanted to be of help to Judie. She'd become unglued; how horrible it must be for her in some foreign land, without her husband. But I was struggling in the world of parenthood right now, which had its own battles, and the only thing I had to offer Judie was a bag of crummy advice. Although she was miles away, I felt that Judie could sense my helplessness at the time, and in doing so, she screamed out of sheer frustration.

"I hate being alone! I'm all alone, Faith!" she yelled.

"Judie, that's not true. You have people who care about you; it's just...look, you have to let go. JT has moved on; you have to move on too. As a matter of fact, I wanted to tell you that...I...I met up with JT's girlfriend at Barcelona. I had a brief interview with her, and I wanted to tell you then. I should have told you then...maybe you would have been in a better state of mind, but—"

She cut me off. "You talked to that woman that night?"

"Yes, but, Judie, I—"

Not allowing me to answer, her voice was grief stricken. "How could you talk to her, Faith? You knew that I was in pain, and instead of consoling me, you go and interview that woman? What kind of friend are you?"

"Judie, that's why I couldn't tell you that night. You were so fragile. I didn't want to—"

"No! No!" she yelled. "You don't care about me, Faith! You're just like all the rest of them; you're just using me, like everyone else. You want to expose me and make a fool of me, and all for what, Faith? Is your precious book that important to you? Why did you choose to write about me, Faith? Don't you know of some other women who are going through the same pain? Or am

I the only idiot that agreed to do this? Maybe you should find some other women to help you write your book so I won't be the only pathetic woman up for debate."

"Judie, you're not pathetic. Infidelity is an ongoing issue that many couples face, and you're right: I should focus on finding other women that are going through the same thing. And you're right: I should have told you about the interview. But I had no idea that JT would be so inconsiderate as to flaunt his new woman in front of you—and on a modeling shoot, of all things!"

I was at a loss for words, yet I tried desperately to speak from my heart. "Look, Judie, I didn't want to write the book at all. I want to help. I know there must be other women out there in pain just like you. I've been there a few times myself. Maybe if we both could work on reaching out to other women, then maybe we could be helpful to—"

Judie was beyond reasoning. Cutting me, off she responded, "Well, you're not helpful. You're just the opposite, Faith: you're hurtful! And I want nothing to do with your book! Or you! Good-bye, Faith!"

She hung up, leaving me in a bed of guilt and shame.

---

# Chapter Eight

The plane couldn't arrive at Portland International soon enough. I was so anxious to run into the arms of my husband. We hadn't seen each other in months. I needed a distraction from this whole ordeal, and Ray had always been the perfect escape. He'd planned the perfect diner cruise aboard the *Portland Spirit*, a classic sea experience with a fine-dining ambiance while the captain provided an entertaining overview on the outside deck, showcasing Portland's main attractions.

"This is just what I needed. Thanks, Ray."

Taking a sip of wine, I breathed in the night air as I watched the scenery sail by. There were children on land, Ray and I waved as we sailed by the Cape Cod–style houses.

"Is everything okay?" my husband asked. "You seem miles away."

"I'm fine."

"You don't appear to be fine. I mean, you look great, but…you seem as if you have a lot on your mind. Is everything okay with Jordan?"

"Jordan is just fine! She misses her daddy, but other than that, she's just fine." Taking another sip, I debated on whether or not to let Ray in on the drama. After all, my husband could be quite attentive at times. He even enjoyed a good Lifetime TV flick every once in a while. Sappy chick flicks weren't a bother to him either. But at the end of the day, Ray was a real man's man. Too much women's drama exasperated him, so I was honest.

"I don't think this is something you could handle, Ray. It's drama for women."

"Oh. Are you and December having issues again?"

"No."

"Then what?" he asked. "I could surprise you. I've always been good at solving all kinds of women's issues. Remember the time I helped you out with finding that new gynecologist?"

"Ugh, yeah." I smirked in a disapproving manner.

"What? I didn't find the best gynecologist in the Phoenix area?"

"Um…yeah, Ray, about that." I paused.

"What?"

"Honey, the gynecologist you hooked me up with frightened me."

"What? You love scary people! Don't you?"

"No, she reminded me of Hannibal Lecter. That was too… weird." Shaking my head, I shook off the horrifying gynecologist memory. "I'll be fine. This night belongs to you and me, and that's how I want it to be: worry free."

"Okay." Reaching across the table, Ray caressed my hand with a tender smile and understanding expression of love and affirmation. He replied, "But if you change your mind, I'm here for you. Remember that, okay?"

"Yes, I know. Thank you."

I loved my husband, a distinguished man, calm, cool, and collected, with salt-and-pepper, distinguished good looks and the charismatic refinement of a classic, award-winning actor. Yet the thing that I loved most about my husband, and which proved to be of great help to my well-being, was his desire to walk with me through times of spiritual growth. This aspect would prove to be both rewarding and challenging throughout our marriage.

# Chapter Nine

Wednesday night brought about my weekly women's Bible study. I hoped that a night spent with my sisters in Christ would shed new light on my broken relationship with Judie. I had come to realize that even some church people I encountered could be just as messed up as ones who lacked faith. Real women and men of Christ don't just study the actions and the peace of Christ; they should also live by faith—not in a way that is holier than thou, but in a humble way. I couldn't quite say that the women in attendance every Wednesday night were at that peaceful place in life, and that included me as well. Now, one particular member who attended was not a believer. Her name was December, and let's just say that back then, I had hope for the woman, until her actions proved otherwise.

There was Marisole, who went by the name Mary. Very talented, she had her own restaurant in the valley. At times she scared me due to the way she would allow her husband, Marco, to rule over her. Now I know the Bible says to honor your husband (Eph.

5:22–33), yet Mary seemed to totally disregard the part in which the Bible commands the husband to love his wife just as he loves his own body (Eph. 5:25–28). Mary's husband cheated on her left and right, yet time and time again, she'd taken him back. Mary relentlessly asked the group to pray for Marco's salvation. Marco was a good-looking guy; he favored the entertaining wrestler known as the Rock, and it was pretty clear that a lot of women loved what Marco was cooking. Marco was a Puerto Rican love machine, but as far as I was concerned, he was a heartbreaker. The way he treated poor Mary was shameful, yet Mary was crazy about her wayward man. She had two beautiful kids by the love of her life, and, of course, her children adored their father; they were much too young to realize that their daddy was an unruly, cheating womanizer. As much as I hated to admit it, I was getting tired of praying for Marco to change! He'd been on our prayer list for a year now, and he had yet to improve. I wanted him off the prayer list for good! The way I viewed the situation was that I had other people I needed to pray for, and Marco was taking up space. If Marisole asked for prayer concerning Marco one more time, I thought I was going to explode!

There was December, who usually showed up to the meetings late and reeking of alcohol. Let's just say that after meeting December's husband, Ebert, I knew she was in need of some deep, spiritual therapy; praying continually was in high demand.

December had married her college sweetheart. They met at Harvard University. December often shared the story of how she had spotted Ebert on campus. He made her laugh. December thought he was attractive and attentive. Not to be rude, but Ebert reminded me of that white guy with the Afro in the movie *Napoleon Dynamite*. Nonetheless, December said it was love at first sight, and from that point on, she vowed to make Ebert Ingram her husband. Once the two met, it was apparent that December and Ebert had quite a bit in common. They both came from influential backgrounds. Both of their fathers had retired from prestigious law firms, and they both had doting socialite mothers who were well-respected in the community. Once the two completed college, they jumped into marriage.

Their elaborate wedding was held in Florida, on Panama City Beach. From there, the young couple honeymooned in Italy. Once their wedding vows were exchanged, the two took no time diving into their careers.

December received her master's in managerial sciences and ended up landing a job as a financial advisor for a well-known firm in Scottsdale, Arizona. Ebert obtained his master of science and doctor of philosophy degrees in chemistry and took a job with a well-known chemical plant in Phoenix, Arizona. Yes, December and Ebert were dinks (double income, no kids) living large. They deprived themselves of nothing, often rewarding themselves through the escape of elaborate trips to Monte Carlo, Monaco, staying at only the top-notch resorts. Ebert, who had an interest in trucks, would spend most of his money purchasing and restoring vintage automobiles, while December enjoyed basking in culture. She loved the arts, and when she wasn't attending a play or ballet of some sort, she indulged in pampering herself, investing her time in expensive spa treatments and R & R resorts.

Eventually, the two relocated to different jobs within the state of Arizona. Ebert had found employment at the same company where my husband worked. They became good friends, and eventually December and I met through the bond of our husbands.

So how did a woman like December, who seemed to have it all, end up a drunk and a member of my Wednesday night Bible study? Well, it wasn't as complex as one would conceive. You see, my husband and I socialized with the Ingrams on occasion, it didn't take me long to discover a disturbing trait about December's dream man.

One evening, my husband and I met up with the Ingrams to attend a play at the Gammage Auditorium in Tempe; it was there that December's predicament revealed itself. Ebert had issues, glaring concerns that annoyed me, and I wasn't even married to the guy. There was only one word that described Ebert to a T: *B-O-R-I-N-G*! Everything about him was boring, from his drab attire right down to his lackluster shoes. Within that brief moment of being in his presence, Ebert spoke of nothing but himself in his nasal, monotone voice. His choice of subject matter was tedious, and his face lacked expression. In fact, the only time he showed any sign of life was when he spotted a monster truck that he liked. He invested in magazines featuring half-naked women sprawled out on top of the hoods of his beloved trucks. He would gaze at these magazines right in front of his wife, and I conceived this trait to be disrespectful.

Don't get me wrong; I'm not saying that guys can't check out a woman or glance at a beauty in a magazine every once in a while. The world is full of beautiful, gorgeous women of all flavors and nationalities, each possessing their own God-given attraction, so a glance here or a glimpse there was usually not a problem for me. But dang, Ebert! I thought. Where is your dignity? His dull eyes practically popped out of his head any time a plastic, centerfold-like woman entered the room. It was difficult to think that December had been married to this guy for going on fifteen years! Ebert was blessed to have her, yet he ignored his wife, who was hungry for his affection. December yearned for Ebert's devoted affirmation. Honestly, I would drink too, if I were forced to hang out with such a clueless mess of a man.

Nonetheless, December had joined our group on the grounds that her husband had become an unexciting fixture in her life. Now granted, I understood December's frustration. Ebert was a lot of work! But on the other hand, December was no walk in the park herself. She really needed to lay off the sauce! It never failed. Every Bible meeting, here came December, bitterly staggering into the meeting late and throwing off the subject at hand, all because her man was a mind-boggling idiot! December herself was getting on my last nerve, too, not to mention that she was now becoming condescending toward me and the other members of my group as well. I should have kicked her out long ago, but I didn't have the heart to do so. I didn't feel right kicking her out of a Bible study for women.

Lord knows, I tried to have a compassionate, open heart toward December. My husband and I even took a vacation with the Ingrams; we flew to Greece, and all December talked about during the whole vacation was how unhappy she was concerning our accommodations. The drinks were watered down, the service was horrible, the food was bland, and so on. Granted, this was my very first vacation outside of the United States with my husband, so I thought everything was great! However, when a woman like December, who builds her life around pleasing herself for a living, goes on vacation, everyone better get ready for an ongoing journey of discontentment!

There was Shelby, a single mom who was in search of a God-fearing man. She had a history of bad luck with men, and now, three children out of wedlock later, she was determined to find a good man with sincere, faith-driven morals.

And then there was Wanda. Short and heavyset in stature, she was a happy-go-lucky, gentle spirit who kept to herself for the most part.

Nonetheless, our meeting started promptly, despite December's being a no-show at the time.

We started with Shelby's blind date. She had met a guy on one of those Christian online dating groups whom she thought would be a perfect match and wonderful father to her children, and the girls and I were dying to hear how things turned out.

"So, how did your date go, Shelby?" Mary asked.

"No comment." She glared. "Honestly, girls, it was a big disaster."

"It was a disaster?" I questioned with concern. I had always heard such good things about those Christian websites.

"Yeah. He wanted to do inappropriate stuff on the first date! He wanted to pull my hair, and that night I was wearing one of those clip-on ponytail hairpieces!"

"Oh no, you were about to lose your clip-on hairpiece?" I gasped.

"Well," she continued, "Toni did a lot of other things that ruined the date. For starters, he was checking out other women. He did not behave like a Christian man."

"Are you sure you met him on a Christian website?" I asked.

"Yes, Christian, but I think as soon as any man finds out I have three kids, they automatically think I'm easy."

"I'm sorry to hear that, Shelby." I sighed. "I tell you, these men nowadays don't have any kind of respectable upbringing. Their mothers didn't raise them properly, and their dads nowadays are out of the picture. And it's not just inner-city children; I'm talking about the suburban kids whose dads are constantly working just to keep an extravagant roof over their kids' heads."

I really felt bad for Shelby, a cute redhead who worked two jobs to support her kids.

I also had concern for Wanda, who always seemed deep in thought. Wanda longed to shed some pounds. We prayed that she would develop the willpower to stick with her diet. However, Wanda was addicted to food, especially chocolate, and at times, it appeared as if the extra pounds were becoming a hindrance.

Nonetheless, her inner qualities and her infectious smile always warmed my heart.

"Shelby, we have to pray for the right man to come along who is sincere in his spiritual walk," Wanda shared. Sighing for a brief moment, she announced, "I have some news to share with you girls. I've been contemplating gastric bypass surgery," Wanda confided. "I think most men are turned off by my weight, and it's not just that." She paused. "I feel uncomfortable. I don't feel healthy anymore."

Mary responded with her usual thoughtful apprehension. "Wanda, you really should research all surgery, as well as the doctors who will be performing such serious operations, before you dive into anything. Your heart may not be strong enough to endure these medical alternatives."

"Oh, I plan to, Mary! I wasn't always this heavy." Wanda smiled in remembrance. "I used to be a hottie! I had a body shaped like a Coca-Cola bottle, just to have you know, ladies. You couldn't tell me nothing—I knew I was fine!" She let out a hearty chuckle. "I was pulling men in left and right."

"Have you considered any healthy alternatives before diving into surgery?" I asked.

"What other healthy alternatives are there?"

"Have you tried dieting and exercising?" I smiled. I didn't want to down Wanda's decision, but I knew from having worked at a weight-loss center that lifestyle is a major part of the process. Many patients who have had gastric bypass surgery have put the weight back on, all due to their lack of desire to change their eating habits and to exercise more. But I have learned to cut my lectures short and try to offer the meat of the revelation at hand.

"The Daniel diet, Daniel 1:8–14. Vegetables are your friend. I need to practice what I preach by indulging in more green veggies myself, I will admit."

"Yeah, I tried," she huffed, "and it don't work." Wanda protested, "The problem is, I love to eat way too much. I can't go to bed hungry, Faith; I just can't live off celery sticks and cucumbers. I'm sorry; that ain't gonna work. I need some meat between my teeth. Yet and still…" She paused. "I'm tired of being over-weight and underappreciated. Maybe this quick surgery will give me confidence once again; but then again, all men are dogs, anyway. It don't matter how good you look. In the end, all they want to do is hit it and scram."

"Don't lose hope, Wanda. Every woman should be in search of a man who is willing to add to her integrity: a soulmate who under-stands what a woman desires!

"He should be a soulmate who's willing to fight for a woman's honor because in her, he finds himself. A relationship such as this would be invincible! It's the way a relationship between a man and a woman should be."

I paused, hating to sound like some sappy Hallmark card, but I was speaking from my heart, and even though the relationship between my husband and me was a spiritual work in progress, we were still striving for that point, which made me confident in my speech on behalf of endurance and patience when it came to seeking the right man.

"I think every woman should set her standards high when it boils down to finding her soulmate, a heroic partner like Jesus."

"Did you say Jesus?" Shelby asked.

"Yes." I nodded assuredly.

"Well, Faith, no disrespect," she said and sucked her teeth, "but I'm gonna be waiting a long time because there ain't no man out there capable of turning water into wine."

I responded, "It's not the miracles performed by Jesus that intrigue me; it's the diligence in dying for love and the grace that he fought for that move me. I desire a man who lives his life out of an understanding that the value of commitment binds."

"I could settle for a King David kind of man myself," Mary confessed. "King David wasn't perfect, but I heard he danced with a lot of passion, and he was a man after God's own heart." She smiled. "Now, you gotta love that in a man."

"Yeah, but he was a cheater," Shelby said. "He had more than one wife, and he took another man's wife; Bathsheba was her name."

"Back then," Mary announced, "all kings cheated and had more than one wife, too! They even had concubines."

I thought to myself, Perhaps that's why she puts up with Marco's cheating ways; maybe she thinks he's one of King David's offspring?

"Well, thank God I wasn't born back in those days, because that type of thing doesn't sit well with me," Shelby responded.

As we continued to debate over the topic, there was a rapid knock on the door. We all knew who it was, and without hesitation I got up to answer it. In staggered December dressed in her usual stiff outfit, which consisted of a navy-blue blazer over a black lace-front camisole; she owned a blazer and camisole in every color. She usually wore black slacks with the pleats near the front pockets and sling-back, open-toed shoes. And then there was that handbag she carried. December loved her purse; it was a big, red, old-lady purse. She'd clench onto those straps like Sophia off that sitcom *The Golden Girls*; she wouldn't let her comfort bag out of her sight.

Despite her stuffy demeanor and corporate-world attire, December had beautiful facial features. Her tiny bone structure strongly defined a fusion of her Swedish culture, and her skin was flawless and beamed with vibrant tones of glistening ivory. She kept her thick blond hair pulled back into a sleek ponytail. On the outside, December appeared to have it all together, but on the inside, the woman was a hot mess!

"Sorry I'm late!" she apologized in her usual frustrated tone as she strode inside, taking her seat next to Mary. To make matters more obnoxious, she had the audacity to start complaining. "Did you guys start without me?"

Mary replied, "Yes, we did, so if you don't mind, we were just in the middle of discussing a meaningful topic."

December rolled her eyes and replied, "Since when has anything meaningful ever come out of your mouth?"

Mary was now upset. "What's your problem now, December? You just got here. Are you really trying to ruin this meeting already?"

December laughed in a taunting manner. "This meeting is a joke."

"Then why do you bother showing up?" Mary asked, getting extremely hot under the collar.

"I really don't know. I keep asking myself that question over and over."

"Sounds like a personal dilemma to me, December, pretty much like all of your problems," Mary replied coldly.

"Isn't that what this meeting is supposed to be about?" December raved. "Aren't we supposed to air our problems in order to help others?" She went on to criticize, "But instead, we listen to you, Faith, and your meaningless babble, and then we wrap it up with prayer to God." She laughed scornfully, looking up at the ceiling. "Where is God? If he's so reliable, why haven't any of us found that special mate yet? Why hasn't he come to rescue us? Tell me that much, Faith?"

I tried so hard to remain calm, but my patience was wearing thin with December. On several occasions December had vented in anger, making it clear that our friendship was only for a season.

As apparent as her proclamation appeared, I didn't want to give up on her. December had some great qualities; she was extremely generous, always funding special organizations in favor of those who were in dire need. Knowing that there was some indication of good within her core, I appealed to her one last time.

"December," I expressed wholeheartedly, "many times, I've found that God refuses to grant us the desire of our hearts because we are not spiritually ready to receive what we ask for, and to be quite honest, there are times when I've thanked God for not giving me what I asked for because, looking back, that outcome would've turned out wrong. We're like children in God's eyes; we don't know what's right for us, so he's protecting us from ourselves."

"Well," December spat, "I'm sick and tired of waiting on this no-show. I'm stuck, and this grim discovery is ticking me off!" she yelled. "I'm sick and tired of showing up to take part in this raggedy mess of a meeting. Just look at you all!" She pointed around the room at each one of us. "You look like a bunch of pitiful clowns sitting around praying." December began to laugh as she pointed at Shelby. "You still looking for a man to play daddy? Please, girl, you got too many kids; no man is going to put up with that!" She huffed. "And look at you!" She pointed in Wanda's direction as she laughed scornfully. "Who would want you? You look like one of those chubby Buddha statues that sit in the entrance of a foreign nail salon. You're so darn huge!" She giggled hysterically.

"Maybe we should all rub Wanda's big belly for good luck!" she mocked.

Wanda was hurt, but she wasn't the type to fight back. Even though she could have knocked December's skinny behind right out of the ballpark, she held her tongue.

Seeing that Wanda was not going to entertain her anger, December directed her vengeful shots at Mary. "And let me guess what we're praying for when it comes to you, Marisole. Hmm… could, it, be your cheating jackass of a husband, Marco?" She huffed. "That man ain't gonna act right—trust me. I got me one of them dogs, girl; they don't change."

Mary stood her ground. "No, actually, I was praying that you would hurry up and get help. You have a drinking problem, and you need to be looking for an AA meeting. You're a bitter woman, so discontent. You think your vacations bring spon-taneity to your life?" Mary mocked. "No, it's just another way to block out how unhappy you are about your life. In the end, you gotta come right back home and face the music: your marriage is mundane." She shook her head in disgust. "Nobody asked you to marry that dry husband of yours, and now you have to drink just to tolerate him. I'm sorry, girl, but you need Jesus more than anybody in this group, because you"—Mary pointed—"ain't nothing but a bitter, lonely woman. Face it, December, you want all of us to suffer along with you, but unlike you, December, alcohol is not my god. It's the master you serve, and look at the results." She gave a reprehensible smirk. "You're the pitiful one!"

December, who had now reached a whole new level of irate sparked by Mary's harsh yet accurate open rebuke, retaliated.

"Don't you dare pass judgment on me, you trifling wench!" She pointed at Mary and then aimed her verbal abuse toward me. "As for you and this stupid meeting, Faith," she said as she staggered toward me, "I know enough about your God to know that you have no right to judge me. You have to tolerate me because you are no better than me.

"How dare you act as if you have no faults when we all know that you, need a J-O-B! You are constantly going out on those dead-end modeling jobs. You need a real joooooob!" she slurred in annoyance. "Maybe Marisole will hire you on at her restaurant. How about that, Mary? Can you stop worrying about that no-good husband for a minute to help Faith get a real joooob?" she spat.

That was all it took. Mary jumped up, bolting toward December, but Shelby leaped up, holding her back as I tried to contain December, who was swinging toward Mary with her granny purse. December, whose anger was jaded by drunken despair, lost her balance and fell to the floor, and her wild breathing gradually simmered down.

I could no longer put myself or the women in such discomfort. I now had to stand my ground and insist that December leave the group for good this time. Taking a deep breath, I announced,

"Look, December, I think it's best if you go home and sleep it off. I'll call Ebert."

"What?" She had the audacity to appear surprised. "You're kicking me out?" she questioned angrily. "That's a bunch of bull!"

Abruptly, I demanded, "December! It's best that you leave! We cannot continue to conduct our group in this disruptive manner. Now, please, let me call Ebert to come pick you up. Or I can call you a cab."

Pulling herself up off the floor, purse in hand, she replied in a bitter tone, "I don't need Ebert, and I don't need no foul-smelling cab driver to take me home. This group can kiss my high-yellow backside!" She slapped her flat bottom as she staggered out of the front door.

After that incident, I never saw December again. Every now and then, I'd attempt to call her when in need of a new hot spot to hit up around town; after all, she was an expert when it came to discovering new ventures around the Valley of the Sun. But I never got the chance to speak to her; her husband, Ebert, always answered the phone. At first I was annoyed, given the whole situation, and I expressed my concern to Ebert over the phone one day; nonetheless, my plea fell upon deaf ears.

As time passed, I accepted and made peace with December's decision to no longer speak to me. December was a woman mentally stuck in a time warp, incapable of evolving in life. To most, December seemed complacent in her misery, an ongoing depression wrapped in a deceptive form of peace. The Ingrams chased after the almighty dollar relentlessly to help maintain their status of comfort in life. I was aware that misery loves company, and the kind of friendship I had to offer the Ingrams could no longer tolerate a false sense of serenity.

When it came to keeping the peace, I preferred to keep it real; however, Ebert and my husband, Ray, remained good friends. I'd often wonder why; after all, Ebert appeared to be just as eccentrically complacent as December, and it bewildered me, the fact that my husband associated with a smug individual such as Ebert, who was set against living vicariously—that is, until I realized that it was all due to Ebert's yearning to maintain a relationship with an individual of total dissimilarity, whose outlook on life was led by faith instead of fear.

———

# Chapter Ten

The time and the place had finally arrived. I had not seen my Latino *chicas* in weeks, and now fate had brought us together through yet another young Spanish designer. After the runway show, there we all stood in the dressing room—everyone except Abella. The need to get the tension out of the air was clear at that point. We stood there, clothed in expensive evening gowns, dripping in custom-made jewelry, batting our fake eyelashes, and doused in dramatic makeup, our hair pulled back in elegant upsweeps, as if we were set to participate in the Miss Universe Pageant; however, this was not the case, and as usual, I was the first to make that apparent. I was tired of faking it. Abella was not there to defend herself. I needed to confront Catalina in Abella's honor.

"How could you treat Abella so disrespectfully, going after her fiancé like that?"

"Oh, there you go! I just knew you were going to start with me! Look, Faith, it was Emilio who went after me! He didn't want

Abella. If it wasn't me, he would have gone after some other woman."

"She's your friend, Cat—and not only that, you're married!"

"I'm filing for divorce. I moved out, and I'm living with Gabby until I can find my own place—and just so you know, Abella and I never got along. I can't stand that girl."

"Ugh! Catalina! Why can't you just do the right thing?"

"Don't stand there judging me, Faith. Get off my case." Cat made her way to the empty station and began removing her jewelry.

"And you, Gabby. Why did you behave like that? The last time we hung out, you acted like a crazy woman! Fausto already thought you were crazy! Behaving like a jealous, irrational woman only proved his point."

"I know. You're right. But I did end up taking off my jacket. I was wearing a really cute blouse underneath. I designed it myself —you really would've have liked it!" She shrugged in embarrassment.

"Gabby! Your cute blouse does not matter, especially after you beat Fausto all upside his head like a punching bag! That's embarrassing, Gabby."

"I know, Faith! Stop talking about it!" Gabby ran over to her station. Sitting down, she buried her face in her hands. "I keep reliving that nightmare over and over again in my mind. I feel awful, and you're right, Faith: I've got to start making good decisions. Fausto is turning me loco!" She began to cry.

"Now look what you did." Catalina turned around. "You made her cry!"

"Conviction does that. I care about Gabby; she deserves better. I have faith that one day, Gabby will make a wonderful business-woman, wife, and mother, but she has to start doing the right thing. If not, I'm afraid that she's going to end up…" I paused, and the look upon my face was judgmental.

"End up like what?" Catalina asked. "Like me?" she huffed. "You just like to make people feel bad, Faith. You're not perfect, but you try to act like you are! You've made mistakes, too, you know!"

"You're right, Cat. I've made plenty of mistakes. I try and learn from them so that I don't repeat these offenses over and over again. I don't want my mistakes to become habits—and bad habits at that. I don't mean to come off like little Miss Perfection, but we have to grow up!"

"Well, I'm doing the best I can, but my best is never good enough; I keep messing up." Cat shook her head helplessly. "I'm pregnant…it's Emilio's baby," she blurted out. "He's gonna stand by me, and that's all that matters." She gave an uneasy grin.

Cat's announcement angered me; I couldn't stand being in the same room with her. Gathering up my belongings, I stormed out of the dressing room. I changed in the public bathroom and left without saying a word.

Some years later, I received a letter from Gabriela. She'd completed fashion school in New York, and she was in the process of starting her own designer clothing store. Gabby thanked me for being truthful and encouraging her to follow her dreams. As for Cat, Gabby told me that she was there for her in the delivery room. Cat had a baby girl whom she named Lilly, and Emilio was a no-show. He wanted nothing to do with Cat or his baby girl, and he was nowhere to be found. Emilio ended up repeating the same transgression that Catalina's dad had committed years beforehand: the curse of abandonment.

As the Holy Spirit dealt more with my heart, I became aware that in some ways I was judgmental of Catalina. I came to realize that Cat was insecure, and her lack of confidence acted out in a disturbing and vulnerable way. Emilio took advantage of this weakness, and through his own insecurities, these two broken spirits encountered one another.

I was proud of Gabby. She learned to be happy by obtaining her goals in life, and she has not married—at least not that I know of; however, she has let go of her cheating boyfriend, who would have become a cheating husband if they had married. Gabriela decided to let Fausto become some other woman's problem, and not hers.

As for Abella, we stayed in touch long enough to celebrate her victory against cancer; it had gone into remission! Afterward, we fell out of touch. Our friendship was only for a season.

———

I was simply annoyed, to say the least! I was receiving e-mails from every angle. Jessie had rounded up a group of women, most of them extremely bitter, and JT, Judie's ex, had rounded up a group of his friends, who were sending in e-mails. They were mostly men complaining about bipolar, beautiful women. Their friends would tell their friends, and before you knew it, my e-mail was bogged down with tons of mail from all over the world. Yet, the one person that I desired to hear from was no longer speaking to me. Not even Jessie knew of her whereabouts. I was stressed, to say the least; so much so that I felt the need to call a meeting with Jessie and JT. Both of them were at each other's throats, bombarding my e-mail account with hateful words toward one another. Not to mention, I'd received an e-mail from JT's girl-friend, Lara, which JT felt the need to share with Jessie because he caught wind through a friend of a friend, who happened to know them both, that Jessie had been talking ill of his new girl-friend—and soon-to-be fiancée—Lara.

I was caught in a coil of ugliness, and I hated it. I had to talk to someone who was of good, sound judgment, so I decided to reach out to a wise friend named Gale. Ms. Gale was quite older than I was. I met her at a church retreat years ago, before I met my husband. Ms. Gale always knew just what to say. I met up with her downtown at a little diner that served breakfast all day: the Good Egg, in Scottsdale, not far from her house. Ms. Gale enjoyed the open-face omelets with golden-brown potatoes and a cup of black coffee. As she indulged in her favorite breakfast treat, I shared everything with her.

As I discussed my position, I noticed that Ms. Gale had not aged as much as I'd expected; her features were still sharp. A couple strands of silver hair intermingled with her auburn-colored strands, highlighting her appearance well. After doing what she did best, which was listening, she delivered her advice.

"Faith is a product of your calling," she said calmly. Knowing that I never understood right off the bat what she meant, she explained further.

"Acting out of faith instead of fear has always been your strong suit. Now that you're backed into a corner, you want to shrivel up and die, throw in the towel, give in…am I right?"

"Yes, I'm scared. I didn't ask for this predicament, but it found me, and instead of making things better, I keep rubbing salt into the wound. At least that's what I feel as if I'm doing."

"Is your intention to destroy the lives of others?"

"No!"

"Well then, there you have it! Act upon your good intentions, and let God discern your motives—not man. Do what you can, and let God take care of the rest, dear. What more can you do?"

Simple but true. What more could I do? And with those words, I was ready to face the music. I was sick of all the "he said, she said" rumors and gossip. So, as soon as I heard that JT was in town, I called a meeting and had Jessie and JT meet me at the Mighty Cup & Spoon in downtown Glendale.

No sooner had I sat down to talk with them both than Jessie decided to vent. "How dare you flaunt that low-class witch in front of my friend? You know what, JT, I was with Judy when you launched your girlfriend's picture on social media; she's hideous! Judie was always way too good for you, JT, and you knew that, you insecure piece of work. You begged me to set you two up."

JT cut her off. "You didn't set us up, Jessie. You might have said a few words to jump-start our relationship, but it wasn't in the cards. Stop acting as if you lost a huge bet in Vegas or something. It didn't work out!" JT yelled in frustration. "Get over it!"

"I'm so sick of men like you! You're just like my ex! All over again! Lies after lies after lies! I'm sick of it! You men think you can get away with any and everything just because you think that you have the right to belittle women! But let me tell you something, buddy: you're a coward!" she screamed.

"And you're a crazy, worthless tr—"

"Stop! Both of you, please stop it! Now this is absurd! I can't take it anymore. Jessie, you have got to find a different outlet for your pain. This is not healthy." Praying for the Holy Spirit to bless me with the right things to say and not be taken over by the hate and animosity that was filling the space, I continued. "Believe it or not, guys, I've always tried to be a person of peace. But in spite of it all, I seem to find myself in the middle of chaos. But you know what? I asked you both here to let you know that if I do go through with writing this book, I'm going to tell the good, the bad, and the ugly aspects of this whole ordeal. So far, there is no right in this whole matter! We all are wrong, and we all failed one another! All of us are failures when it comes to showing peace and patience, love, kindness, and the biggest victim out of this whole matter is love. If you think that I'm going to present a one-sided documentary, then you're both wrong. I want to write a book that's going to help women and men grow from their mistakes. I want to write a book that will move a person to at least strive to do the right thing out of love, not selfishness. So you two can stay here and fight amongst yourselves, but I'm done.

"And one more thing, might I add: stop sending me e-mails! This forum is over!"

And with those words, I left, and I was happy never to hear from Jessie or JT ever again.

---

# Chapter Eleven

I had found out through credible sources that JT had gotten married; nonetheless, his marriage to Lara only lasted for a year. She caught JT having an affair with her fitness trainer. According to close sources, Lara ended up hurling a chair at JT's mug; no serious injuries resulted from the chair assault. I don't know what it is about JT, but it appears as if women enjoy throwing food and furniture at the man. I think he better watch out, or he may end up messing around with a woman who has good aim.

As for Jessie, she served time in jail for assaulting a male clerk at a local convenience store. I can only hope that her bitterness toward men has died down, but that's really all I can do, is hope.

I didn't know what to do with the information I had or how to present it, so I started by launching a website and posting some of their e-mails on the site. Back in the day, blogging was not as popular as it is in today's culture. I let everyone know that they could view most of the comments on the site that I created. I was able to find a swimsuit model named Aiva to share her story, but Aiva was not as humble as Judie, which made it somewhat difficult for the public to embrace her pain. I do realize that not everyone deals with the subject of infidelity the same way; some women are sad, like Judie, and others become bitter, like Aiva.

I'd hoped that I would see Judie once again, and many years later, I got that chance. While I was waiting for my agent at a trendy new Italian restaurant that had just opened up in downtown Phoenix, I spotted a healthy, wiser-looking Judie having dinner with what appeared to be her new husband, an older, distinguished gentleman who genuinely showed public signs of affection toward her. Every now and then, he would reach over and lovingly caress her arm. They both were wearing wedding bands, but what warmed my heart the most was the small child who sat playfully between the two of them. The young boy had his mother's discerning eyes. I overheard her calling the toddler "Tristion" as she knelt down beside him, picking up his sippy cup, which had fallen off the high chair. She lovingly stroked his curly auburn locks. As if she could feel someone watching her, she spotted me across the room. We exchanged a brief smile of acknowledgment, both of us knowing that our friendship was only for a season; nonetheless, it was good to see that Judie's prayers were finally answered.

Years later, I heard from Judie, who wasn't happy with the responses posted on my site. She wanted her voice to be heard, so she sent me a lengthy letter via snail mail. The return address showed that she was residing in San Diego at the time. Within her manuscript of words was her forty-day journal, which she had used as a coping tool to get through her hardship.

I found out that Judie had gotten out of the modeling industry and had planned to go back to school to become a nurse, in hopes of someday working in the children's ward. She shared that the world did not need more models; instead, she wanted to become a role model for women, letting them know that they don't have to be the victim. Her journal reveals that she had made quite a transformation!

Judie gave me permission to share her journal in this book. Judie's journal presents questions that she felt were an important part of her healing process. Judie wanted to share her growth with other women who were struggling with trust issues due to unfaithful relationships. In addition, I have added words of wisdom, as well as room for readers to write down their own answers concerning their personal journey.

---

In 2011, the debate book was released under the title *Why Do Married Men Cheat with Unattractive Women?* This book covered the viewpoint in a forum style of writing similar to blogging, leaving space available for others to partake in their own forty-day journal; after all, I thought, who would be interested in reading Judie's journal? Apparently, many women—as well as a few men—can identify with Judie.

The next chapters are from the debate book; they cover feedback concerning Judie's story. A few other women who have faced trials similar to Judie's have also been added into this forum. Feedback from all angles of infidelity is followed by Judie's personal forty-day journal, adjacent to words of affirmation.

Maybe Judie is onto something. After all, in the end, Judie found her happily ever after, a goal that many women may be in search of.

---

# Chapter Twelve

*The Debate*

*I Can't Believe He Cheated
with That Unattractive Woman!*

When I found out that my best friend's husband was unfaithful, I was shocked!

After all, my attractive friend (whom we will call "Judie") is a gorgeous model—and she knows how to turn heads.

I was with Judie when she discovered the other woman's picture online, and…how can I put this? The other woman had a face that only a mother could love. It was visibly noticeable that this woman was out of shape—and not by a couple pounds, mind you!

The other woman was a brick community house! She also had bad skin and had obviously missed a couple trips to the dentist.

The other woman simply did not take pride in her appearance. To be honest, I was a little disappointed to see the results. I had figured if Judie's husband cheated on her, then the other woman must have been drop-dead gorgeous!

Sadly, I got to wondering, why do married men cheat with unattractive women? Eventually, I asked Judie's now former husband what made him cheat with the homely chick. He explained that the other woman made him feel good about himself; Judie expected too much of him. This charming other woman was eager to please him, both physically and mentally.

He went on to say that she showered him with compliments all the time, important gestures of the heart that he claimed Judie never showed.

In Judie's defense, I know that if her husband would have simply told her what he expected from her, she would have gone the extra mile for him.

I have come to realize that this issue has no boundaries. Even Hollywood stars have fallen victim to this bizarre case. We have all witnessed Hollywood wives whose husbands have ditched them for unattractive or even less successful women. Insecurity may very well be the cause of most Hollywood breakups.

In obvious cases, when a man leaves his wife for a woman twenty years younger, he is consoling the urges of his midlife crisis, and the other woman finally has the dad she always wanted.

However, in the case of the man who leaves his swan princess for the ugly duckling, he is now considered the poor guy who needs to console his insecurities.

And now the unattractive woman can brag to all her friends about how she stole Barbie's husband.

*Signed,*
*Judie's Friend till the End*

# Chapter Thirteen

*The Response*

Is being beautiful, attractive, and able to turn heads the real key to a successful marriage? If so, why are Hollywood couples constantly in divorce court?

Honestly, it appears that guys have no idea what they want. Men say that they desire women who present a "challenge" and play hard to get; so, if she is not a challenge, men become tired.

However, they also want a girl who is affectionate, loveable, puts him first, showers him with attention—but then they get bored because she is not a challenge.

I think the bottom line is that guys want as many women as they can possibly have. This is not a complex issue.

*Signed,*
*Honestly*

Men do what we allow them to do, ladies. The signs are there; we just choose to ignore them. The man cheated down. Big deal; let him go, and expect less in your next relationship.

*Signed,*
*Truth*

Would it have made Judie happier if the other woman was attractive? Personally, I would've felt better that he downgraded and couldn't find another woman that could take my place. So far, my husband has been faithful—but I am his third wife.

*Signed,*
*Southern Peach*

"In Judie's defense, I know if her husband would have simply told her what he expected from her, she would have gone the extra mile."

Are You Kidding Me?

You don't know this for sure. Why should a man have to tell his own wife what he expects from her? A wife should know how to please her own husband.

*Signed,*
*My Outlook*

The reason why Judie's husband cheated with the ugly girl is because she did things that the pretty wife refused to do. The ugly chick lived up to his fantasy.

Judie's husband has always wanted to do freaky things, and Judie would never try. And then this new girl comes along and will do anything he wants.

*Signed,*
*Honest Harry*

---

To Judie's friend, please understand that looks are not important. Judie's physical appearance is not enough to keep her relationship going.

Beauty is now a procedure that anyone with money can obtain. Inner beauty is priceless.

*Signed,*
*Royalty*

---

It appears that inner beauty is more important to Judie's husband than external beauty. The other woman is obviously a more caring and loving person and therefore seen as more desirable than your physically attractive friend that YOU find to be beautiful.

*Signed,*
*Victorian Beauty*

Most likely, the reason why men cheat with unattractive women is only due to a lack of sex, but also caused by a lack of emotional encouragement. I am not saying that the action of cheating is justified. It doesn't matter if the woman is attractive or not.

*Signed,*
*The Average Woman*

---

It's not uncommon for a man with insecurity problems to cheat down. Judie's husband is the type of man that will usually single out a weak, unattractive, abandoned, and even elderly woman. The other woman made him feel important, desirable, and loved.

His affair has nothing to do with anything that Judie has or has not done. The problem with Judie's husband is that he needed to "feel good about himself."

This type of affair committed by Judie's former husband is called the "Selfish Affair." He is not thinking of his wife, nor is he thinking about the other woman...only of his own selfish concerns. In these types of situations, the "other woman" is thrown away like a heap of garbage. Judie's husband does not want to leave his wife; he just wants that emotional feeling of being desired. Don't we all want to be desired?

Most confident, established, and intellectual men find other ways to work it out with their wives. Infidelity is a weak and irresponsible way for a man to handle his insecurity issues.

*Signed,*
*A Beautiful Soul*

---

I was/am the other woman! Men like Judie's husband would have emotional affairs with me. I know why married men cheat with unattractive women.

What is missing in Judie's "irresistible, perfect relationship"?

Judie failed to take care of her husband's psychological and emotional needs. Judie needed to become his friend, someone to whom he felt comfortable opening up his soul. Judie expected her former husband to be perfect. Perfection is a high expectation to live by. Can anyone truly fit the bill?

*Signed,*
*Juicy Details*

---

It's not an insecurity issue, as Judie's friend wants us to believe. Where was the honesty in this relationship? Why should the man feel that he has to be the strong one? As men, we must hold our own and become strong, brave, and cater to women. Women expect this from us. Why should the emotional strength to hold a relationship together fall on the man? Women, you have to do your part, which is allowing us men to feel vulnerable at times. If not, we will fall into the arms of another woman—which I should know because I cheated. My beautiful wife was shocked. I am sharing my side of the story with you abandoned, beautiful women. Please take note.

"Judie expected too much of him. In Judie's defense, I know if her husband would have simply told her what he expected from her, she would have gone the extra mile for him."

Judie's husband felt that his wife "expected too much of him," not what he expected of her. I have studied that a lot of men cheat when they lose that emotional bond and look for it else-where, and it is not based on how a woman looks as much as it's the emotional part of being content. Women assume men cheat just because of the sex and looks. Studies have shown it's more about the emotions of a man; looks don't have a lot to do with this matter. I have had the most beautiful women as girlfriends; I had to adapt to their drama, and their striking attractiveness wears off, then the emotional becomes the most important thing. I am dating a woman right now that society considers to be unat-tractive.

When people look, she sometimes questions her appearance due to her facial blemishes, but her heart and ability to care for others I find to be truly amazing! The depth of her inner beauty makes her very desirable to me. When I am with her, I feel special.

So your friend Judie is a drop-dead gorgeous model; big deal. This means nothing to men who have already been with a model. It's the men who haven't been with a beautiful woman that often think that looks matter. Unfortunately for Judie, her looks were not enough to hold on to the man she loved. The cheating part is uncalled for; however, I understand why her husband cheated.

*Signed,*
*Dillon*

---

Without hearing from Judie's ex, we don't know the full story. Here are some thought-provoking answers.

Beautiful women can be "needy." Some I've dated lack confi-dence and are consistently seeking constant validation. Beautiful women need to hear that they are attractive on a daily basis. This can become exhausting!

Most likely, Judie's ex found someone with whom he could share a sincere emotional bond.

Over the years, Judie could have taken some "things off the dish" that the ex needed, and the new woman was open to such pleasures.

To Judie's friend, I find it inadequate that you accused all men who leave their wives for younger women as going through a midlife crisis and that younger women suffer from daddy issues. Women and men cheat for different reasons. It does not mean that we are going through a midlife crisis.

Looks have nothing do with it. You simply can't help who you fall in love with.

*Signed,*
*Roger Out*

---

Aviva, a swimsuit print model standing five feet ten inches in height, with beautiful high cheekbones and chiseled facial features, vents:

It's extremely disturbing when I have done everything in my power to stay fit, watch what I eat, and undergo intense beauty regimens—only to have my husband cheat down on me with a woman who looks like a hobbit. At times, I would catch a glimpse of my husband gazing at short, stocky, manly-looking females. I thought he found them to be unusually fascinating. Now I find out that my husband is physically attracted to this type of woman, which leaves me to wonder if this is the kind of woman my husband desired all along; if so, then why did he marry me?

His actions have truly humiliated me! My feelings are beyond hurt. I took our marriage seriously. There are plenty of attractive men who approached me as well, and these men looked way better than that unattractive hobbit he ran off with. I was devoted to him, and this is the thanks I get? He is truly pathetic!

# Chapter Fourteen

*Who Are You Calling Unattractive?*

"A face that only a mother could love"?

How shallow can you be? You should be ashamed of yourself. Is that all you care about is looks?

Do you really believe that looks are what kept your friend's relationship together?

In case you have forgotten, it was "Beauty" that killed the Beast!

*Signed,*
*Ms. Unattractive!*

---

I'm not a good-looking guy, Aiva. Yet, I have dated some of the most beautiful girls in the world. I'm not a fool; I know most of these women are after my money. Yet and still, I can entertain these beautiful women because money is what money does: it, too, is in the eye of the beholder.

*Sincerely,*
*J.S.*

———

Aiva, you would have had a harder time with your husband's infidelity if the other woman was more attractive than you.

I am not unattractive, but my husband ended up leaving me for a woman that was 12 years younger, beautiful body, tall, and she had more attractive features than me.

I was hurt even more because now I feel as if my husband will never see me as being as attractive as her, and I find it very hard to be myself without feeling like I have to compete physically and emotionally. I was not good enough for him.

Judie, feel better that the other woman was less attractive than you; otherwise, you would have had more insecurity issues to confront, as well as dishonesty.

*Sincerely,*
*Broken Queen of Hearts*

———

To all of the people who have commented on Judie's sexual performance in the bedroom as one of the key factors leading to why her husband cheated with an unattractive woman, I find these statements to be ridiculous.

"Because Judie is a gorgeous model, maybe she can't satisfy him!" or "Judie is egotistical!"

Listen, people: in spite of what Judie did or did not do, that was his wife, and he had a responsibility to tell Judie what he expected of her! None of us have heard from Judie. None of us are in any position to judge her.

The only one that is self-absorbed is Judie's former husband because he is the one that cheated with that unattractive woman!

*Signed,*
*Darci*

---

Honestly, I am the other woman that men cheat with. I don't like being called unattractive. Who are you calling unattractive?

Are you saying that just because married men cheat with someone like me, that they are insecure?

I'm not as conventionally attractive as his wife, but for some reason he stays with me.

He probably cheats on his wife because women like me know how to compliment a man, and we pay more attention to their men, more so than their ATTRACTIVE WIFE!

*Signed,*
*Short & Sweet*

---

Aiva, looks are not everything. I know many women that have been cheated on, and these are butt-uglier women. I think men would rather be happy with an unattractive girl than unhappy with a beautiful model. I think that sometimes attractive women think that they don't need to work hard to keep their relationship intact; they think their looks will compensate for all of their hang-ups. But they don't realize that men want other things, too, besides a beautiful face and perfect body. Live and learn, Aiva!

*Signed,*
*Butt Ugly Woman L*

---

Aiva, you may think that you are attractive, but obviously you are not attractive to your husband. "Attractive" people can't hold a relationship together. "Unattractive" people are better at relationships because their ego is not in the way.

My friend is a model, too. The woman can't hold on to a relationship to save her life!

I have another male friend who is a dog-face cheater! He cheats on his beautiful wife because he "enjoys being the male slut that he is." He did say that the other woman makes him feel good. I guess men cheat to feel loved.

They all get on my nerves! Men are such liars!

*Signed,*
*Aubrey*

# Chapter Fifteen

*There Is No Excuse for Cheating!*

Aiva, I am sorry to hear about this!

Marriage is hard work, and both parties need to stay alert! Guys like a challenge and a supportive woman. If he is not getting it at home, he will find it somewhere else. Trust Big Daddy. Make sure you follow your natural instincts, and don't ignore the warning signs. If your man was a cheating ass when you met him, he will probably be a cheating dog later.

However, you probably do need to get freaky in the bedroom; most models are kind of stiff in that department. I speak from experience.

Most beautiful women have a hard time in the bedroom. The reason being is that sex has nothing to do with beauty.

*Sincerely,*
*Big Daddy*

Judie, your former husband is the scum of the Earth. There is no excuse for cheating! My husband cheated on me 11xs—once with my own sister. We had four kids together. He never took me out. I felt so ugly, I was miserable. In a sad way, it's comforting to know that you pretty models and movie stars get treated the same way. Deception is a curse to us all.

*Signed,*
*Margret*

---

Men cheat with women who make them feel better. That's their excuse, and we just have to accept it. I have been married to my husband for 17 years, and he cheats like a rabbit. I'm tired of it; I don't know what else to do but let a dog be a dog.

*Signed,*
*Ann*

---

It takes two to foxtrot! Judie, did you bother to go the extra mile? Did your former husband really ask you to go the extra mile?

*Signed*
*Ms. Curious*

---

Aiva, when a woman steals your husband, there is no better vengeance than to let her keep him! My husband cheated on me, too, and I'm glad he's gone! The two idiots deserve one another.

*Sincerely,*
*Loral Lee*

---

Whatever issues this man had, he had prior to meeting Aiva. And these issues were tested by marriage. Oftentimes, people do not know who they are before entering into a deep relationship. And when things unavoidably become dark, they realize that they "desire" for someone to make them feel good about themselves. That's the issue right there! Why do you "need" someone to fill in your voids?

Why can't men just be honest about their feelings? They have to hide behind an excuse that bears no dignity whatsoever. There will never be a logical reason for cheating. There is no excuse!

*Signed,*
*Ms. Diana Jones*

---

I have been a pastor for many years. And yes, my faith teaches me to honor my wife in marriage. I want to keep my promise to God, but a funny thing happens when men plant goals to do the right thing in life. Commitment happens!

I could never hurt my wife. I want to help her, not hurt her. Because when she hurts, I hurt. She is my rib, and I love her! God gave this woman to me to protect her, not to harm her. And in return, she becomes my helper.

My prayer for all women that have been betrayed in life is that soon you will find a man that loves you as he loves his own body. This is what you deserve.

"But a man who commits adultery lacks judgment; whoever does so destroys himself. Blows and disgrace are his lot, and shame will never be wiped away" (Prov. 6:27–33, NIV).

*Sincerely,*
*Pastor Thomas*

# Chapter Sixteen

*I Can't Stand Beautiful Women!*

I guess it's your turn now! Tell me, beautiful woman, how many times have you heard that you are not so pretty? Your man is getting something that you were not giving him at home.

Judie, I take issue with your stupid friend that an older man will go for a woman half his age to fulfill the "daddy" issues—this is totally not true. It works for Hollywood couples, and it works for me.

Obviously, Aiva, you are dumb as a log and a self-absorbed supermodel, and all along your man wanted a real woman. Like me!

*Signed,*
*Unattractive Like Me!*

---

Is that all you gorgeous models have to offer is your "beauty," Judie? An airheaded bimbo is what you are. I'm completely against infidelity, but I believe your husband should have left you, Little Miss Perfect, instead of cheating. But maybe he was tired of your drama! I can't stand beautiful women! You all make me sick with your fake attitudes.

As the saying goes, "When you see a beautiful woman, just remember somewhere there's a man who's tired of her drama!" Beauty fades, Beauty Queen!

*Signed,*
*Lance*

---

Once again, another beautiful woman fails to make her mate feel loved. And what do they do? Turn to the media so we can all feel sorry for the famous model. Shut up with your whining and take a class, Aiva!

*Signed,*
*Frankie*

---

Aiva, the other woman offers your husband more love. She appreciates him. She doesn't nag about helping with the chores, she looks past his mistakes, and she probably tells him he's a hard worker. The other woman knows how to please him sexually.

AIVA! YOUR LOOKS WON'T KEEP YOUR MAN!

*Signed,*
*Whatever!!!*

I must admit, I'm rather enjoying this. I have been pushed around by beautiful women all my life. I never thought for once that beautiful people get dumped on as well. My ex-girlfriend was a model. She took off with some guy and moved to Spain—but not before cleaning out my bank account and wrecking my car, which I'm still paying for. I'm now living with my brother. He warned me to stay away from beautiful women, that they're nothing but trouble. I found out the hard way. To be honest, right now I'm fed up with all women—even the ugly ones.

*Signed,*
*Benji*

---

Aiva, I am so sorry, this is not about being pretty or not. This is about true love. Why is it that unattractive women are not allowed to find love with a "handsome" man? Are we less human because we don't look like Hollywood wives? I just have to say the ugly duckie women are twice as affectionate as the swan women. I am not defending unattractive people because I am unattractive. I am defending these "unattractive" women because they are humans just like everyone else! Sorry to whoever wrote this—you are heartless!

You must be a fake Hollywood woman as well.

*Signed,*
*Dina*

How sad that this world is so shallow. Judie's friend, you are very sad. I am one of those "unattractive" girls, and ya know what, I would rather be ugly and a nice person than a shallow, mean, "attractive" girl. You and your friend are just shallow, mean, and I find your attitude to be unattractive!

*Signed*
*Bialy*

---

Aiva, your husband left, because you have fake Barbie bleached-blond hair and fake Bozo the Clown lips. Don't you get it? He wanted a real woman! And apparently, once you get rid of all that fake stuff, underneath you will find an unattractive woman like me.

Who would have thought? I can't stand beautiful women!

You get away with everything in this world just because people think you're nice to look at. This is too funny. Everyone thinks that beautiful women are worth more than gold. When in reality, your own spouse can't stand you!

*Signed,*
*Give Me A Break!*

---

Hey, Aiva, I guess you got a wake-up call: looks don't matter at all! Sometimes, beautiful women just need to get a clue! Maybe when they realize that their poop stinks, too, they will change their attitude!

## Memoir of a Jaded Woman

My husband left me for a beautiful woman. When is my book coming out? Let me guess…in the year 2000 and NEVER—that's when! Because the world does not want to hear about an overweight woman who got dumped by her husband! The world only wants to know about rail-thin models and movie stars! Forgive me if I don't shed one tear for another famous person. Your husband dumped you because you have no brain cells. There! Problem solved! NEXT!!!

*Signed,*
*Kiss My Attitude!*

# Chapter Seventeen

*My Husband Cheated with an*
*Unattractive Woman!*

My husband cheated on me with an ugly duckling. He was a complainer. He was always too ill, too exhausted from traveling.

When I was fed up with his whining and told him to get over it, he found a big, fat, ugly circus clown to whine with. You should see how much makeup this barn cow wears. It's ridiculous.

My husband's affair worked in my favor because now I don't have to look at his stupid face.

*Signed,*
*All Men Get On My Nerves!*

---

My husband cheated on me with a plain-looking woman. However, he did me a favor. It was strenuous to deal with someone who was sucking the life out of me without giving anything back.

At times, I miss being with someone. However, it was too painful to be in this relationship. I'd rather be alone than suffer in pain.

*Signed,*
*IDGI*

---

Judie's friend, who are you to determine if this woman is attractive or not? She only needed to be attractive to YOUR friend's husband—not to you, his wife, or anyone else.

At least you can't call him shallow, only interested in "attractive" women, and unable to recognize spiritual beauty.

*Signed,*
*Into Unattractive Women!*

---

Aiva, did you expect your man to pamper you? Wake up! Men have feelings and emotional needs, too! You left that out there, and now I bet you have deep regrets.

*Signed,*
*The Hobbit*

---

My wife and I have been married almost 30 years, and there has been infidelity on both sides, but we realized what was important and have worked on fixing our problems for the last 10 years—

which, by the way, have been the best years of our marriage. Marriage takes work, Aiva.

You're young; you will learn.

*Signed,*
*It's Cheaper To Keep Her!*

---

As a woman who has been cheated on, I have a few things to say. When I found out about my husband's affair, I thought I was going to die. We had been married for 12 years. He told me about his affair, and all I could do was sit there in disbelief and listen to what he had to say.

This woman was also not attractive, according to my friends, who were obviously trying to make me feel better. Personally, I found her to be attractive.

He told me that she listened to him and told him all the right things that made him feel like a real man. He told her about the way I treated him. My husband's words were hurtful. He wants to come back into my life. But I can't trust him.

*Signed,*
*Hopelessly Out Of Love*

---

Judie, men will screw around with any woman that will have them.

Perhaps with the so-called "unattractive" other woman, your husband has the upper hand on things?

Maybe your husband cheated to annoy you and your STUPID girlfriend, who took the time to look the other woman up online?

*Signed,*
*Wasted*

---

Aiva, my husband cheated with a woman who has 5 kids from 5 different men.

I had a better career than my husband, better job offers, and I was more successful.

He eventually left the other woman who had a heap load of children and started sleeping with a girl I can't stand! My ex, and your ex, are both weak pieces of COW MANURE!

*Signed,*
*Love Hurts!*

Aiva, your husband is just a scumbag, like any other man that cheats. Doesn't matter if the unattractive woman made him "feel better" about himself, he's still a DIRT BAG idiot for cheating. My husband cheated on me, too! I keep myself up, go to the gym, jog, watch what I eat, and then this idiot goes out there and has an affair with a woman that was built like a linebacker for the NFL! I was like, "Hold up... wait a minute!" That man has lost his mind. He left me for some raggedy mess, for sure. That's on him. 'Cause I'm not gonna ever let that two-timing cheating lowlife crawl back in my bed—never!

---

Unattractive women are ugly because they cheat with married men! My husband cheated with my sister. They both lack moral values. I find their actions to be unattractive. I am still in shock over this careless affair.

*Signed,*
*Polly*

---

Cheating is caused by lack of communication. We need to communicate—that is what a relationship is all about!

*Signed,*
*Miss Communication*

---

My husband cheated with an ugly duckling, and I can tell you that my head is still messed up over this. I now have a void that is never filled. Men, if you are even thinking of cheating, please stop and think about your wife and the "other woman" and start treating your fellow sister as you would want to be treated. Stop being pathetic! Talk to your wives; we want to work things out. Do the right thing in your relationship. One day, it could be your daughter that you may have to console.

Is this what you want? Your kids will be affected by your dumb affair and shameful sin! Is this what you desire? Think about the lives that you are destroying.

*Signed,*
*Wisdom*

From my personal experience, my husband ran off with a very unattractive woman, and it lasted 1 year. He told me about 7 yrs later that I expected too much from him. All I expected was love, and I always made him feel special, but I also wanted a full commitment. He said the other woman expected nothing from him, just a good time, and he liked that for a while. Aiva, I found out later he cheated on every woman he was ever with. I have now found a man who is wonderful and who's not afraid of commitment. Just have faith! Faith conquers all!

*Signed,*
*One Day At A Time!*

# Chapter Eighteen

*The Other Woman Speaks Out*

I am the other woman. I am the woman that is now dating Judie's ex. It's unbelievable the responses this topic has received, and I am annoyed by it. I guarantee that the only reason why people are so intrigued with this story is because a beautiful model is involved.

If I would have dragged my homely, fat behind out there and complained that someone had stolen my husband, this issue would have been straight up ignored. I'm sure comments like "Lose some weight, ya big heifer, and maybe your husband will come back to you!" would have been the end result.

I am truly sick of the world we live in. The way that we perceive the images of others is shallow. The girl next door, the all-American girl, sweet and petite—none of these cute descriptions describes me. And it used to bother me, but not anymore. I'm not ashamed for having an affair with Judie's husband, although I probably should be a bit remorseful—but I'm not. There is a certain satisfaction that I have in knowing that I stole Barbie's boyfriend. There, I said it. The fat whore scores big, right? Please, we would not be having this conversation if I were skinny and beautiful.

To Judie's friend who insulted my appearance, yes, my face breaks out; I work at a burger joint, and being around grease causes my face to break out. But I guess you wouldn't know anything about this because you are a stay-at-home Barbie. You don't need to work for a living.

I also enjoy eating and cooking; big deal. And as far as my teeth are concerned, I may not have freshly bleached piano teeth like yours—however, I do go to the dentist on a regular basis, thank you very much.

Why do I cheat with married men? Honestly, I don't like commitment. I'm from a household where commitment never existed. I enjoy cheating with married men. I do what I want with them, and then send them home. I can't stand having affairs with men who have children because kids are needy and those relationships don't work out. Men who don't have any baggage/kids have more freedom.

Judie's husband came into my restaurant one day. He told me he sneaks away every so often to grab a burger because his wife is a vegetarian and can't stand meat. On this certain day, he had forgotten his wallet, so I hooked him up with a free burger. And that's how it started. The way to a man's heart will always be through his stomach. I'm not sure where this relationship will go, but I'm in it to win it. I actually like this relationship.

Do I feel sorry for Judie? Absolutely not! I know I am a home-wrecker, but it takes two to cheat. A word of advice to all married women out there: a cheating woman's worse nightmare is a faithful husband.

*Signed,*
*Burger Queen*

# Chapter Nineteen

*Judie's Ex Speaks Out*

I am not one to judge on whether a woman is ugly or not. My mother always taught me to respect a woman based upon her actions. My ex-wife, who you all know as "Judie," was and is a beautiful woman on the outside; however, she has mad issues on the inside.

I am a photographer. I have captured beautiful women on film from all over the world; however, many models that I have dealt with in the past have huge hissy fits, similar to the tantrums of a two-year-old child. I feel that oftentimes spoiled celebrities/models rarely hear the word NO. They are constantly given everything they desire, making it impossible to try and please them.

On one occasion, Judie threw a hamburger at me. She was upset because I had forgotten that she was a vegetarian. This vision of beauty also threatened to poke my eyes out with the pointy end

**121**

of a chicken skewer. To make matters worse, I was sex-deprived, verbally, and mentally abused. Again, when I met the other woman, she made me feel good about myself—and she knew how to cook. If any of you guys out there have ever dated a model, you know that the majority of them can't cook, and when they do…well…the attempt alone is grounds for divorce.

I believe Judie's unhealthy diet was the cause behind her insane mood swings. I seriously believe Judie was hungry all the time because she refused to eat properly. I tried to save my marriage. Judie wanted to write a book about the pitfalls of the modeling world. She felt that this would bring closure with whatever it was she was dealing with. I supported her wishes, and everything was going well, but her mood swings got worse concerning silly stuff. One day, Judie had another one of her dramatic model melt-downs—because she has to be the center of attention at all times. I could not take it anymore, so I packed my bags and left.

When I enter a room with my new girlfriend, I feel that I am being acknowledged as well. Even though she is not considered beautiful according to the standards of this world, she makes me feel beautiful, and in return I am able to genuinely love her.

I can't pretend to know why some married men cheat. I never thought I would be in this category; however, at the end of the day, a man wants to share his life with a woman that treats him respectfully.

Trust me, the more beautiful the woman, the more hoops you have to jump through.

*Signed,*
*JW*

# Chapter Twenty

*Men Speak Out*

I hear ya, man. If she can't give it up in the bedroom, leave her. Find someone who makes you feel appreciated. Beautiful women are hard to handle. What you said is true! The more beautiful the woman, the more hoops you have to jump through.

*Signed,*
*Brad*

Beautiful women are an emotional mess! And what good are they if they can't cook?

They're only good for one thing—and they can hardly accomplish that job either.

*Signed,*
*Carson*

Beautiful women are overrated! Stick with the ugly ones; they behave more respectful.

I cheat on my woman, and she lets me get away with it because she knows she can't do any better. I know this sounds bad, but it's true. As long as she puts me first, I'm going to take advantage of her.

I have trouble with pretty women; they think they are better than me or something. Maybe I take the rejection out on my fat housewife.

I really can't stand women. They all need to stay in the kitchen and learn how to cook.

*Signed,*
*Redneck & Proud!*

---

I can't stand beautiful women. They have nothing to offer but a foul load of baggage and tears and more tears.

I don't understand why they exist? Is it to keep the malls in business?

All women spell trouble! Even the unattractive ones!

*Signed,*
*Forget About It!*

---

I do not know why men cheat at all. To be honest, I hate men who cheat on their wives! It makes me sick. I adore my wife, and I would never cheat on her. I have a problem just talking to another woman; I do not want my wife to think that I am the least bit interested in someone else. Having an affair is the worst thing you can do to your wife!

Men, when we make a vow, it is between US AND GOD! Why are many of us breaking our vows? Are we really this weak over women who get off on destroying our relationship with the bride that God gave to us as a gift?

The number #1 deal breaker is a man who is committed to his marriage!

*Signed,*
*Committed till the End!*

# Chapter Twenty-One

*Judie Speaks Out*

First of all, please allow me to address the hamburger incident. The reason why I threw a hamburger at my ex is because on the night of my birthday, he did not show up until 1:00 a.m. He handed me a hamburger and refused to tell me where he was. I was upset. It was obvious that he was out there having a burger with that other woman when he should have been home with me. My former husband kept coming home late. Upon his arrival, he had a strange odor within his clothing, similar to the smell of canned meat—it was disgusting! I found it extremely difficult to have sex with someone who smelled like Spam. In regards to the chicken skewer, that never happened. I don't eat meat; why would I walk around with a chicken skewer?

I am shocked that many people love to see models suffer. I am appalled that most of the concern is in favor of men who have chosen to cheat on their wives. My husband vowed to love and honor me till death do us part. Many people attack models, calling us stuck up, self-centered, shallow, bimbo, and whore; I don't understand. To make matters worse, some people comment that the reason why men cheat on us is because we are not freaks in the bedroom? How do you know what goes on in our bedrooms? Are you a fly on the wall? And to the women that indicate that models have no brain cells and we only care about our looks, this is not true! Why are we the hated ones? These men are the ones who cheated! Why are we now forced to wear the scarlet letter?

I vowed never to cheat on my husband because I come from a background in which my dad constantly cheated on my mother. My mother would allow him to come back time and time again. I swore to myself that I would never be the other woman and that I would do everything in my power to try and please my husband. I went the extra mile. I tried with all of my heart and soul. I tried hard to keep my marriage together.

My ex cheated because he is insecure. I tried to help him by giving him words of affirmation. Obviously, he did not enjoy my cooking, so I took cooking lessons.

I know what it is like to feel insecure. As a kid, I was awkwardly tall and constantly picked on by my classmates. The taunting was so extreme that my mother took me out of school and I completed my studies at home. Most of you think that models lack feelings. I have feelings! The majority of men that approach me are married. I reject their advances because through my mother's pain, I know what it feels like to be cheated on. When a man cheats, not only does he betray his wife, but he hurts his children as well.

In my lifetime, I have only been approached by two single men. One turned out to be gay, and the other one ended up cheating on me.

Which leads back to the topic concerning my ex-husband, the one that has the majority of you all fooled. I tried many times to get my ex to go to church with me; he went one time—and fell asleep.

He obviously missed the sermon on adultery that day.

I stand behind my girlfriend's statements. I don't believe my ex-husband's girlfriend is ugly due to her appearance. This is my friend's opinion, which she is entitled to have.

We all have commented negatively on one's appearance at one time or another. "Let He Without Sin Cast The First Stone."

Would you all prefer that I send the other woman roses with a card attached, thanking her for ending my marriage? What would you do in my shoes?

I believe the other woman is ugly because she committed an ugly act by having an affair with my husband.

I loved my husband, and I wanted to start a family with him.

There is nothing more I can do about this situation. To my friends who supported me through this difficult time, thank you! I would also like to clarify that I am not writing a book on the pitfalls of modeling; my ex made that up as well. Letting go is easy. Forgetting is the hard part.

*Signed,*
*Judie*

# Chapter Twenty-Two

*Move On!*

Judie, I threw a steel-toed boot at my ex. The same thing happened to me, and people were so cruel. You will do better, Judie! Just move on!

*Sincerely,*
*Carole*

---

Judie, what your friend should have said is that women who cheat with married men are ugly on the inside. Time to move on! I can tell you want to go back to him, but please don't. Move on! I speak from experience. Let him go.

*Sincerely,*
*Jamie*

---

Judie, I know how to cook—and my husband still left me. It really does not matter if you can cook or not. But I encourage you to continue with your cooking lessons; practice makes perfect. Who knows, one day you could end up with your own cooking show!

*Sincerely,*
*Joanna*

---

Judie, I cheat on my wife left and right. Nothing can change this —not church or kids. Nothing can change the urge that a man feels inside. Some people may think that I am evil for telling you this, but this is the truth. Nothing can change this. So your husband smelled like canned meat. Do what you have to do to please him in the bedroom; this is what matters. I'm only being honest with you because I actually feel sorry for you. You really don't seem to know what happened to your marriage.

Lust happened, Judie.

*Sincerely,*
*LL*

# Judie's Forty-Day Journal

I was in a very bad place in my life when I decided to write this journal. For starters, I'm a very private person, extremely shy in character; many may wonder, how can someone who makes a living confidently walking down a runway scantily clad, be shy? It's simple, modeling was my escape, I was able to shed my shy persona, and transform into a more confident person. However, deep down inside, I knew that I was not that confident girl, and that eventually, I would have to transform back, into my own reality, which was a lonely place to be.

I was told that I lacked enthusiasm and zeal. So, I guess I tried to gravitate toward people who owned this quality. And that's when I met my husband Jonathan.

When I found out that Jonathan went on to marry the woman that tore our marriage apart, I fell into a deep depression. Unable to eat or sleep, I cried until I ran out of tears. My eyes burned in sorrow.

My friends told me, "Judie, you're a beautiful woman, and there's a world full of men. You can choose any man you want." The only problem was, I didn't want just any man, I wanted the right man.

It's very hard for others to understand a person like me. I've always felt different, almost as if I never belonged on this planet, from day one. I look around, and everything appears foreign to me. No place felt like home. I could be on a shoot in Brazil, or right here in America; regardless, I felt out of place, lost, and lonely. The best way I can describe my private pain of inadequacy is that of a person living inside a snow globe; I'm watching everything take place in a whirlwind of confusion, yet I'm standing still, plastic, dead, just watching the others around me live their lives immune to the chaos which surrounds them.

When I was young, and sometimes even now, the least bit of attention mortified me, especially if it was negative. When JT left me for that other woman, my greatest fear gripped my heart: a panic of not having a purpose in life. I knew that if I did not do something to free my soul from this curse, I would die a slow death inside.

Journaling seemed to be the answer at the time; it was actually my last resort. By sharing my journal, I hope that others will have the courage to move on, in faith, knowing that everything will work out in the end.

At first I felt vulnerable writing about my feelings and my shortcomings; I feared that someone would find my journal and taunt me. But then, I thought, my ex has already made such a colossal fool of me—what more do I have to lose? I encourage every woman to break down the wall of vulnerability, and write down your words that are hidden behind the barrier of fear.

# DAY 1

*Do You Value Marriage?*

Today I pondered the question as to whether or not I valued marriage.

Like every little girl, I dreamed of one day marrying a loving man. Growing up in a dysfunctional household made me eager to define the meaning of true commitment. I was determined that if I were ever to find the right man, I would work hard on valuing the relationship. I haven't found that right man yet, and sometimes I wonder if I ever will. After all, how can I value a union that seems destined to end in divorce?

I now believe that marriage devalues me.

---

*Grow stronger in the face of pain (faith has your perfect mate in mind).*

*Faith of Peace*

*Break down the walls of vulnerability, write your thoughts.*
*How do you define marriage?*
*A union, bound by the creator, of adoration.*

## DAY 2

*Are Your Parents Still Married?*

Today I pondered how my parents' relationship may have affected my interactions with men. My parents are no longer married, and after witnessing what my mom went through in order to try and maintain her marriage, I was put off by relationships for the longest time, in fear that I, too, would face the same hardship that my mother had faced for years. My mother was madly in love with my dad; however, it was evident that my dad did not share the same passion. I could tell by the way he treated her.

If Dad felt the same way about my mother as she did about him, they would have remained married; I'm sure of that. I often wondered, *Am I destined to share the same fate as my mother?*

———

*(Do not dwell on the failed relationships of your parents; this is a dealing of the past. God created a brighter future, by creating you.)* Grace.

*Faith of Peace*

## DAY 3

*Did Your Dad Respect Your Mom?*

I often wondered why my dad didn't respect my mother. I couldn't find the answers, so I made the mistake of asking my mother—major mistake. Mother thought I was picking on her. I wanted to know how a man could marry a woman, only to disrespect such a fragile being in the end? I would've asked my dad, but I don't know of his whereabouts; he ended up leaving my mother for good. I was ten years old when my dad left my mom and me.

I often wondered if I was the reason why my dad left?

---

*You have a perfect father, one who surpasses all earthly knowledge. A father who adores you, and embraces all of your flaws.*

*Faith of Peace*

*Can you define respect?*
*Admiration valued through trust.*

## DAY 4

*Did Your Mom Respect Your Dad?*

Did my mom respect my dad? A little too much, if you ask me.

I remember my dad came home with a present for my mom. She was so ecstatic. My dad had trouble holding on to a job, and it was usually my mother that would work cleaning houses, and as a seamstress, to support our family, so the one time my dad was able to hold on to employment, he brought home a random gift for my mom. Dad gave my mother an electric can opener! After years of my mom being the sole provider for our family, that's all the guy could come up with, an electric can opener? I wish she would've thrown it at him, but no; instead, my mother acted as if it were the best gift that she'd ever received in her whole entire life! My mother worshiped my dad, and in return, he left. How's that for respect?

---

*God will not allow abuse. But if you are not careful, a selfish man or woman will! Don't allow your controlling spouse to rule over your life as a divinity. You can only serve one God.*

*Faith of Peace*

*What is your definition of a good relationship?*
*A connection that grows through the power of everlasting love found in*
*patience.*

## DAY 5

*Do You Prefer Long-Term Relationships?*

I prefer a strong relationship—period; however, sometimes I can tell right off the bat that most of my relationships are not going to last, so why draw out the inevitable? I prefer long-term relationships in hopes that someday they could lead to marriage.

Lately, I feel as if I've been chasing potential mates away, in fear that it will lead to disaster. I find myself behaving poorly. Recently, I'd gone on a couple blind dates; two to be exact. The first guy kept sneezing throughout dinner. He said he had bad allergies. I'd wished that he'd taken an allergy shot or something, anything, to stop the constant sneezing. It seemed as if he were allergic to everything! His eyes began to swell up, so much so, that he resembled a strange looking bug-eyed fish, by the time [the date] ended. I felt bad for the sick guy, but I couldn't see myself with this man for one minute longer, let alone in a long-term commitment; no, it was awful. Just…plain awful.

The second man I went on a date with spoke entirely too loud. He said he was hard of hearing. He owned a sports bar, which explained the reason why he couldn't control his polluted mouth —and not to be rude, but he had this strand of hair, just one long piece that kept swaying back and forth under the vent; it was very distracting. I'm so frustrated, but I think it was just too soon. I honestly don't know what I prefer anymore, and why should it matter, when the outcome remains the same? Utterly disastrous.

*In time, all good things come to pass.*
*Don't lose hope.*
*Faith of Peace*
*Are you in favor of a long-term relationship?*
*Surround yourself in a relationship of peace.*

## DAY 6

*Do You Have or Desire to Have Children?*

I would love to have children. I even thought about adopting, but I didn't want the child to be without a dad. My dad, he was in my life for a short while, but not really involved in my life, if that makes any sense at all. Anyway, I would like a house full of kids! It may seem like a fairy tale, but I grew up as an only child, and I was so lonely. I often wished for a brother or sister to play with. But nowadays, I can barely find a man that can take care of himself, so what good would a child do in that kind of situation? I don't want to have a child with a man in hopes that he'll grow up as soon as the child is born. I need a man that has outgrown his infancy.

---

*If a man or woman behaves like a child, then expect to experience an immature journey!*

*Faith of Peace*

*Define growth?*
*The expansion needed to grow in wisdom.*

## DAY 7

*What Did You Dislike about Your Childhood?*

What I disliked the most about my childhood is that I felt invisible. My mother tried to be attentive, but she had to work. Soon, I became comfortable with the notion of being unseen. When my dad left me and my mother, she focused her attention toward me; now, instead of the need to try and please my dad all the time, my mom began badgering me. I'm sure my mother meant well. It was her that forced me into modeling, always bragging that she was nothing like me as a child, and she'd often boast about how outspoken and charismatic she was. My mother said my dad was the same way, outgoing. She found it odd, so to speak, that such a timid child like me could ever exist. Modeling mortified me. I guess I got used to being indiscernible; growing up, at least then, I could daydream and observe the world around me without discernment.

---

*No matter how inadequate we may have felt as a child, God always cared for us, seeing us through to adulthood, just as he cares for the lilies of the field.*

*Faith of Peace*

*What is childlike faith?*
*Pure love, which overcomes all hate*

# DAY 8

*What Did You Like about Your Childhood?*

What I liked about my childhood? The only fond memory I had growing up was hanging out with my grandmother. She'd take me to church. My grandmother attended a peaceful church, and everyone was just as fond of my grandmother as I was. My mother used to say that my grandma was way too strict on her, and then when I was born she eased up a bit. But my grandmother's love toward me felt genuine, and she was wise; everything that came out of her mouth held a certain truth and understanding. It's hard to find someone that speaks the truth nowadays without being offensive. I miss my grandmother, and someday if I'm blessed enough to have children of my own, I pray that I can give words of wisdom as well.

---

*A wise person will tell you the truth in a gentle manner. Whether you can handle the truth is a whole different matter.*

*Faith of Peace*

*Are you a person of perception and empathy?*
*Wisdom and understanding surpass all ignorance.*

## DAY 9

*Have You Ever Cheated on Your Spouse?*

I never cheated on my ex-husband. Despite how awful he treated me at times, the thought never entered my mind. I was determined to make a difference in my marriage. I never understood when a woman or man would say, "My parents cheated on one another, so that's why I cheat." Don't we owe it to ourselves to make a difference in our own marriage?

---

*No man is without fault, but the individual who strives to keep peace within his core will conquer lust, which is the enemy of good will.*

*Faith of Peace*

*Do you fight against temptation?*
*Through the actions of faith, good seed is planted, producing the power of love.*

# DAY 10

*Do You Think about Cheating on Your Spouse?*

The thought of cheating on my ex-husband never entertained my thoughts; however, I'd been approached a number of times by other married men while I was married to JT.

The proposition that stands out in my memory came from a photographer from Italy. Of course, I cannot reveal his name, but this individual attempted on several occasions to tempt into having an affair, despite my telling him that I was married. What I found to be odd was that he, too, was married, to a beautiful French model. He went so far as to have his wife meet up with me in a public venue in New York. It was there that she insisted that I sleep with her husband. Apparently, they were swingers. He thought that her approval would change my mind, but it didn't. I have strong morals. How can what I dream of having most of all, a marriage built on honesty, ever transpire if I carry myself in such an inconsiderate manner? I thought for sure that my then husband, JT, who was a photographer as well, would never stoop to the level of this photographer. But, I guess I was wrong.

---

*Find a man who is committed to his moral values; not in a creepy cult-like manner, but in a sense that brings peace to your heart!*

*Faith of Peace*

*Is thinking about cheating a sin?*
*One should never entertain the thought of infidelity; impure thoughts develop into lustful desires.*

## DAY 11

*Why Do You Think Married Men Have Affairs?*

Insecurity is the reason why I believe most men have affairs. However, I can remember one day while I was on a shoot in London, bawling my eyes out…and I guess the photographer was fed up with my tears. It was cold and threatening to rain, and he really needed to get through the shoot in a timely manner, and I was being difficult. My divorce had just been finalized, and this weighed heavily on my heart; nonetheless, the photographer, who knew of my predicament, had enough of my tears and shouted, "Look, love, I heard about your divorce, and my heart bleeds for you. If the bastard was standing here, I'd smack him one, good and hard, just for you. But you need to clear up the tears, sweetheart! Men cheat! That's what they do! And most women deal with it. I'm sorry if this is news to you, but we got to get through this shoot, because you're beginning to annoy my sensitive side."

Well, the photographer was right: accepting infidelity was news to me. Nonetheless, we got through the shoot, running mascara and all.

---

*Even though the world makes wrong seem right, hold on to your integrity; eventually, you will encounter the right mate, one who shares your meaningful values dear to his heart.*

*Faith of Peace*

*Why do men cheat?*
*Fighting temptation is a part of life, a battle that conquers the cheating male.*

## DAY 12

*Why Do You Think Married Women Have Affairs?*

I think married women have affairs to get even with their husbands. But in the end, I know that getting even through infidelity serves justice to no one. Sadly enough, a woman or man who behaves in this manner is only stooping down to the level of humiliation. It's not in my heart to compromise my moral convictions.

---

*Most women yearn for affection; they have an empty void that they are unable to fill spiritually.*

*Faith of Peace*

# Judie's Forty-Day Journal

*Why do women cheat?*
*The flesh is week, and the spirit is hungry.*

## DAY 13

*What Is Your Definition of "Insecure"?*

At times, I feel like being a model is the definition of insecurity. Constantly striving to meet the physical standard of a client, doing whatever they ask, whether it's changing your hair color or losing more weight. I wish I was secure enough to tell them all to shove it! But...I'm not. I fall into the make-believe world of perfection, in turn setting a false image for young girls who dream of being just like me.

---

*My definition of insecurity is not having the belief to have faith in a purpose higher than yourself.*

*Faith of Peace*

*Define insecurity?*
*When fear overpowers faith.*

## DAY 14

*What Is Your Definition of "Secure"?*

My definition of secure is finding someone to love me for me. I haven't found that yet. But I'm still searching.

---

*As humans, we seek to obtain love; most of us are born with this gift, which is designed to be shared.*

*Faith of Peace*

*What is love?*
*Love is sacrifice.*

## DAY 15

*Have You Ever Been Deceived?*

I've been cheated on multiple times. The greatest betrayal of them all was committed by my dad. Our first recollection of what faithfulness should stand for should be visual within the relationship between our parents. At times, I feel that my dad set the stage for my ongoing issues with men. But to be honest, I'm tired of being mad at my dad. Because of his unfaithful behavior, I am now in search of a man who is devoted to love.

---

*How faithful is the Lord, unyielding enough to meditate upon your tears. He is your first love, unmoved in the face of deceit.*

*Faith of Peace*

*Define deception?*
*Deception fears the truth.*

## DAY 16

*How Do You Define the Word "Trust"?*

I define trust as being solid in the truth. I would never want to break that commitment, and in return, I expect the same honesty.

---

*Trust is being dependable, without fail! We all have failed. Failure, is a flaw, which makes us human.*

*Faith of Peace*

*Define trust*
*Reliance that one day, doubt will be replaced by faith.*

## DAY 17

*What Makes You Feel Insecure?*

What makes me feel insecure is rejection. I often wonder when it will cease, this ongoing roller coaster of inadequacy.

––––––––––

Insecurity shows its deceptive face when you worry about your place in this world, how others perceive you, or if they notice you at all. Run the race that is placed before you as only you can!

*Faith of Peace*

*Define security.*
*Protected from fear by faith.*

# DAY 18

*How Would You Describe the Perfect Woman?*

My definition of the perfect woman is a woman who is able to hold on to the perfect man. Obviously, that is not me, because I can't hold on to any man, and I have yet to find the perfect one.

However, today I met someone who I'd seen before in the past. He sets up the props on location. I heard that he also designs movie props as well, for motion pictures, but his real love is designing furniture. It sounds odd, but today he approached me. He doesn't have much hair, but he's strong, very well built, and he smells nice, like fresh wood. I know this may sound unusual, but I like the smell of fresh wood. Growing up with my grandmother, we used to take long walks down a windy dirt road that led to a turquoise-colored lake surrounded by fir trees; the smell was consoling to me. This guy reminded me of that fond memory. I'll just say that I prefer the smell of fresh wood over canned meat. L At any rate, he asked me out. I'm not sure if I'm up for it, but I'm considering. Being around his woodsy scent makes me feel uplifted. I love the smell of fresh wood. I hope that's not creepy.

---

*We all fail when it boils down to being the perfect man or woman. But, we can say that we serve a perfect Creator who loves us in all of our weakness.*

*Faith of Peace*

*Can you describe perfection?*
*Companionship, a perfect friendship that is beautiful within its own timing.*

## DAY 19

*How Many Single Friends Do You Have?*

I have way too many single friends to count. I wonder if this could be part of my problem. Hanging around too many single people could send off a negative vibe. The single girls that I hang around with are always complaining, and I think it could be rubbing off on me. I don't talk much; I just sit around and listen, absorbing up all the negativity. Perhaps I should go out with that guy I met. I call him Mr. Woodsy because he smells like a fresh forest right after a refreshing spring shower. I think about him a lot. I think I may call him. It's either that or my single friends. Um…yeah, I think I'll give Mr. Woodsy a call.

---

*We all were single at one point in our lives. None of us came out of our mother's womb engaged to be married, so hanging around single people doesn't mean you're heading down the wrong path, but you do want to try and hang around an uplifting and faithful group.*

*Faith of Peace*

*Define true friendship.*
*Promise bound by secure loyalty that is void of all indifference.*

# DAY 20

*How Many Married Friends Do You Have?*

Come to think of it, I only know of one married couple, and I hardly see them because they have children.

---

*Marriage is a commitment that takes a lot of work, an ongoing endeavor to become one element against all odds, without tearing apart.*

*Faith of Peace*

*Define unattractive.*
*Distasteful conduct, lacking in* commitment.

## DAY 21

*What Is Your Definition of an Unattractive Woman?*

My definition of an unattractive woman is a woman who has an affair with a married man and then boasts about her infidelity as if she's won the lottery.

---

*An unattractive woman is a slave to immorality. Everything that is wrong is right in her eyes, as long as it serves her purpose alone. RIGHTEOUSNESS is her enemy.*

*Faith of Peace*

*Define integrity.*
*Having the wisdom to fight against deceitful measures.*

## DAY 22

*What Is Your Definition of an Unattractive Man?*

My definition of an unattractive man is a man who brags to his friends about an affair that he had with a waitress at a fast food restaurant, then brings home a burger to his vegetarian wife on her birthday.

I know I really have to get over my ex-husband, and I will. He may have broken my heart, but now it's up to me to mend it. I refuse to spend the rest of my life fuming over that unattractive man!

---

*An unattractive man is a slave to immorality. Everything that is wrong is right in his eyes, as long as it serves his purpose alone. INTEGRITY is his enemy.*

*Faith of Peace*

*Define perfection.*
*Excellence, revealing itself in God's perfect timing.*

## DAY 23

*How Would You Describe the Perfect Man?*

Well, I'm sure Mr. Woodsy is far from perfect; however, he is quite the gentleman, I'll give him that much. To be honest, I never knew what the perfect man was. I never developed a clear vision, thanks to my dad and what's-his-face! But now I have a description to work by, thanks to Mr. Woodsy!

I ended up going out with the rugged, slight-peach-fuzz, balding guy with a nice build. He actually prepared dinner at his house. He asked me what I liked to eat, I told him I was a vegetarian, and he prepared the most delightful meal all by himself. Now mind you, I'd never gone to a man's house before on the first date; even when I went out with Jonathan, I declined. Early on, Jonathan had invited me to his penthouse, and even though I liked him, I did not want to come off as being easy. I was sure that Johnathan had entertained plenty of models back in his day, and I did not want to be one of them.

However, things were different with Mr. Woodsy. Meeting up with him at his house was a first for me. I actually felt safe around him.

When I arrived at his creek-side, timber-style home, as he called it, he had a candlelight vegetarian dinner prepared! A spread fit for a vegetarian queen. Stuffed red onions with brown rice and herbs, minted pea watercress soup, Thai fish cakes, and angel-hair pasta with prawns. And for dessert, hot chocolate fondant cake! In the cozy surroundings, I felt at ease. I was surprised to find out that Mr. Woodsy is a couple years older than I; however, he appears much older. I'm not one to question why anyone looks older than they should, because that would be rude, but I guess he suspected I was thinking along those lines when he revealed his age. He looked as old as he did because he's lived a very hard and stressful life. I didn't mind, though. He had the surroundings that made one feel as if they were enjoying a warm evening at a discreet and quaint resort. I like Mr. Woodsy; he makes me comfortable in my own skin. I like the fact that I can sit and listen to him. He didn't talk dirty toward me or try and persuade me to sleep with him. He was the perfect gentleman, and I didn't blush, not once. I'm ashamed to admit that I'm shy. I can honestly say that I'm a woman of very few words. I really do believe that I was born to be more of a listener and not a speaker. I am mortified by the notion that one must have an opinion of the other upon meeting. The only opinion I have is in regard to me and the close friends that surround me, which are very limited. I feel that we are who we are due to our personal circumstances. With time, I truly believe that no individual remains the same. I don't understand reality TV, nor am I a fan of online forums or blogs; they all sound so contemptuous and judgmental. Why would anyone subject themselves to that? I thought by sharing my feelings I would gain understanding, but everyone turned on me; at least that's how I felt. Sure, I got some positive feedback, and I feel awful that those who came to my defense were stricken like they had the plague due to their transparency.

I will say this: I spent a lot of time observing meaningless conversations, and for once I shared an evening with someone I feel I could listen to for the rest of my life. Mr. Woodsy spoke to me as if I were a voyager eager to learn about incredible, new, and exciting wonders in life! I like that about him! Sure, there may come a time when our conversations may turn old, but the way I figure it, if I spent this much time observing and listening to a bunch of nonsense, I can surely spend my future golden years perceiving and focusing on behavior and expressions that are enlightening! I think the perfect man should make a woman feel perfect in her own skin, even when we, as women, are far from perfect. By finding the right man, we should all come close to excellence, perhaps? J

---

*Praise the Lord! For it is he who gives every woman a good man and creates a new song to sing. Abandon the old melody in order to hear the innovative harmony.*

*Faith of Peace*

*Define desire.*
*The need to fill a void that hungers for love starts within the core of your being.*

## DAY 24

*What Do You Desire out of a Relationship?*

Again, I don't know what I desire out of a relationship. I think I've been waiting all this time for a man to show me. Sure, some women say a big diamond or a nice, fancy car, but where does that leave a woman who can provide all of those things for herself? I desire something more, but I know that whomever I am destined to share the rest of my life with must yearn for the same necessities as I do.

---

*A man and woman know if they have found the perfect relationship or not. They will either run from the truth or jump into a lie. If it is the wrong relationship, their differences will form into a yoke\* around their necks that will be unbearable to haul.*

*(\*Yoke: a wooden crosspiece that is fastened over the necks of two animals and attached to the plow or cart that they are to pull.)*

*Faith of Peace*

*Define relaxation.*
*Comfort can be hard to grasp in a life; it is threatened by ongoing drama.*

# DAY 25

*Why Do You Think the Divorce Rate Is So High in America?*

I think the divorce rate is so high in the country due to selfishness. We all want things done our way; no one is willing to bend for the other, in fear of domination.

I can remember when I had just entered into the modeling industry. I was young, barely seventeen years old. I had booked a job for a well-known company that specialized in chic clothing for young women. When I showed up, the coordinator was livid. She began raving that she'd requested a model that was fully endowed on top with dishwater-blond hair. She told me that my pictures were deceiving and that I looked nothing like my comp card. The makeup artist scrambled to embellish my breasts and found a blond wig for me to wear. When the shoot was complete, the executives were not happy. They were disappointed and said that I looked like a whore in disguise; that's what they actually told my agent. So I had to go back in my original state and shoot again, which ended up pushing back the campaign date. Why do we have such a hard time accepting an individual for who they are? In a split second, we can divorce our spouse because they've put on a few pounds, or perhaps we found someone who fits our needs a little better. America makes it way too easy for us to have things our way. We can simply disregard the traits we no longer desire.

The sad thing is that most of the time, there are children involved. What are we teaching our kids about commitment?

---

*Make sure it is truly God's union behind your marriage, and not lust. Get married for the right reasons—RESPECT!—and the rest will follow. It is impossible to stay married to a person whom you don't respect. You may say, "I respected this man," or, "I valued this woman when we got married, but after the marriage, she started misbehaving." Trust me, there were tell-tale signs in the beginning; you just chose to ignore them.*

*Faith of Peace*

*Does divorce represent failure?*
*In certain circumstances, a divorce can be freeing if the marriage was never liberating to begin with.*

## DAY 26

*What Is Your Definition of "Faith"?*

My definition of faith was hidden behind the deception of fear. When I got divorced, I feared that everyone would talk about me or pity me. And they did. But through faith, I became strong enough to move on in search of a new day.

Faith is the willingness to persevere through mundane, unfair treatment in a fast-paced world, striving toward a brighter future. Faith reveals itself first in the mind, in the body, and in the soul. Faith gives birth to the unseen, making it visible for all to see.

————————

*Faith of Peace*

*Define comfort.*
*Everyone needs compassion reassured with peace.*

## DAY 27

*Do You Trust Easily?*

Do I trust easily? Not anymore!

Today, Mr. Woodsy and I took a long walk near the Santa Monica Pier; it was during our walk that I confided in Mr. Woodsy about longing to get out of the modeling business. Even though I was establishing a name for myself here in California and New York, in spite of my age, no longer having to go on a go-see or attend any cattle calls, I felt empty inside. Most models try and venture off into movies, but as for me, I was growing tired of the early schedules and traveling around the world, leaving no time to take in the world around me. I was just tired. Mr. Woodsy asked me to come work for him. I couldn't picture myself wearing a tool belt, trying to chop wood or read blueprints, or whatever it is that one would do as a prop/furniture designer. But he said he could find something special for me that he was sure I would enjoy. It all sounded wonderful, but I've trusted too easily in the past, so this time around, I wanted to be sure, and I will try to pray about it—if I can remember how to pray.

---

*Once trust is broken, it is hard to gain it back, but remember that peace can restore what darkness has struggled to steal away.*

*Faith of Peace*

*Define trust.*
*Faith that moves mountains.*

## DAY 28

*Has Anyone Ever Taken Advantage of You?*

Of course I've had people take advantage of me, and I've accepted the fact that this is how the world works. We come in as trusting children, and through the selfishness of others, we end up cynical and closed minded, all due to broken trust.

———

*I have learned to give without expecting anything back in return; this consists of my time, money, or possessions. I do so in a way that does not force a person to depend on me or put me in need of their affection toward me. Trusting God leaves no room for disappointment.*

*Faith of Peace*

*Define order.*
*Categorizing your life to make room for peace is deeply needed.*

## DAY 29

*Do You Forgive?*

I'm working on forgiving my dad and my ex-husband, but it's hard to do so when neither one has bothered to ask for forgiveness. I feel as if I am the one to blame, the presence of unforgiveness taunts me, causing me to muddle in darkness.

———

*My dear friends, this is easier said than done. I have failed in this department plenty of times. Forgiving is very important; it's forgetting the offense that is the hard part. Call out to God to help you do so as many times as you need, and do not let your pain plant a bitter root in your heart. But most important of all, move on! Do not wait around like a sitting duck in fear of another attack.*

*Faith of Peace*

*Do you have trouble forgiving others?*
*Forgiving is easy; forgetting is a trial within itself.*

# DAY 30

*Can You Define Forgiveness?*

Can I define forgiveness? Apparently not. My ex-husband called me today; it was the first I've heard from him in months. He said he called to find out how I was doing. Can you believe that? Apparently, he'd just gotten married to that woman, and now he's calling to find out how I was doing? Then he goes on to ask, would I be frequenting the beach house we shared together in Maui? Ugh! The nerve of that man! JT makes my skin crawl. I kid you not, I started breaking out in a rash along my forearms. I told him to take the house and never call me again. Once the paperwork was faxed over, I removed my name from that house and changed my number. That house was way too expensive anyway. JT will never be able to keep up with the payments, not on his salary combined with that of that fast food worker he married. I hate to trash her profession, but uhg! You know, what's the purpose of forgiveness if the person you keep trying to forgive keeps infuriating the situation? How many times must I forgive?

---

*Forgiveness is freeing yourself from the chains of bitterness. Forgive as many times as it takes for you to liberate yourself from the stronghold of anger.*

*Faith of Peace*

*Are you broken?*
*A broken heart stays shattered until the victim is strong enough to pick up the*
*pieces. Healing is on the way! Moving on fuels the power of forgiveness.*

## DAY 31

*Have You Ever Broken Someone's Trust?*

I don't believe I've ever broken anyone's trust. I don't have very many friends. The only person I've ever let down is myself.

---

*Learn to address your motives, the reasons behind your actions; broken reliance is often provoked by fear.*

*Faith of Peace*

*Can you move on?*
*Letting go is easier said than done. But it is possible, one day at a time.*

## DAY 32

*Have You Forgiven Yourself?*

Have I forgiven myself? Probably not. Perhaps I should work on doing so. Even though I desire to move on, I find myself looking back, unable to trust my own decisions. Sometimes, I lead myself astray.

---

*Grant yourself forgiveness. Head on toward grace!*

*Faith of Peace*

*Define being single.*
*Being single is a necessity in times of revelation and honors self-fulfillment*
*that embraces the purpose of an all-knowing power.*

## DAY 33

*Do You Mind Being Single?*

I've spent so much time being by myself that I've become eager to find the right man. I enjoy spending time with Mr. Woodsy. I don't like being alone. Who does?

---

*I don't know of any individual who likes to be alone all of the time. Perhaps the mother with a house full of screaming kids may find enjoyment by hiding herself in the bathroom for a moment of peace. Nonetheless, alone time is needed in order to make room for the right person in your life. Too many distractions end up clouding God's awesome purpose for your life. Who wants to end up on a path of uncertainty? Embrace your single life for now; if you can't stand to be by yourself every once in a while to meditate on your thoughts and to strengthen your faith, wisdom lack the power to grow within you.*

*Faith of Peace*

*What hinders your life?*
*Move on in search of peace.*

## DAY 34

*Do You Find It Hard to Move On?*

Apparently, I do find it hard to move on, according to the man I'm now seeing. He shared that I have a problem letting go of JT, and that on several occasions, I'd vented over him. The new man in my life told me that if I wanted to move forward in our relationship, I'd have to leave my ex-husband behind. This was probably our very first argument, because I felt that I had every right to be angry. Yet, I had to admit that Mr. Woodsy was right; he wasn't rude or condescending when making his point. He shared that if I was truly at peace, then I needed to allow peace to take over my life completely.

Deep down inside, I knew that I needed to move forward; after all, JT has.

---

*Letting go allows us to move on into the freeing power of peace, which holds open a new chapter of blessings.*

*Faith of Peace*

*Describe the perfect date.*
*The perfect date is your divine appointment with faith.*

## DAY 35

*What Is the Perfect Date?*

Today, Mr. Woodsy and I took a stroll on the beach. We watched the sunset; it was breathtaking. Again, the conversation was warm and sincere. I now know that the perfect date doesn't have to be acted out in extravagance; the perfect date is being in the presence of someone you value.

---

*Many times, the perfect date can be a spontaneous appointment reserved through devotion.*

*Faith of Peace*

*If you could travel anywhere in the world, where would you go? Create your own world of peace.*

## DAY 36

*If You Could Live Anywhere in the World,*
*Where Would It Be?*

I used to think that if I could live anywhere in the world, it would be somewhere breathtaking, near the ocean. So, when my ex-husband and I purchased our oceanfront property in Maui, I thought for sure I'd be happy; whenever our marriage faced adversity, we could just take off to Maui! I came to realize that there are some issues that not even nature can fix. I now desire to live anywhere peace resides. And so far my wish is to be with a man who honors peace and well-being. Through faith I have found the right man; his name is Christión, a.k.a. Mr. Woodsy.
♥

---

*Flourish in the midst of adversity. Let God guide your steps, He will lead you to victory.*

*Faith of Peace*

*Define prayer.*
*Something that we all need but most rarely do*

# DAY 37

*Do You Pray?*

I'm starting to again. I used to pray a lot when I was a child; for some reason, it was easier to do. But as I got older, life started happening, and I couldn't find the time or the peaceful space to do so. Now, I have found the time and the space, and I have come to a point in my life where I can't afford not to pray. It's a part of me, a necessity, like the air to breathe.

---

*To pray is very simple. One may say, "I don't believe in prayer," but on the contrary, most likely you do so every day, either in your thoughts or through a hopeful desire rooted deep within your heart. You may pray through your tears while hiding away in your closet or bathroom. Prayer doesn't have to be a big production; prayer can be short and sweet or deep in meditation. An effective prayer is spoken from the spirit, and as with everything in life, whether you're exercising, trying to find your core, or studying for a big test, grasping for understanding and results takes time. Granted, you don't want to go around town talking to yourself; instead, find a quiet place, go to the park, invest in your own journal, search, meditate, and believe—all without ceasing! Through childlike faith, exercise the privilege of prayer.*

*Faith of Peace*

*Define prayer.*
*A request made known to a higher power found within the desire of your*
*heart.*
*I challenge you to write down your prayer request, and don't forget to mark the*
*date. God is not a genie in a bottle; sometimes* no *could be his answer, but in*
*the end, you will find, that He was always- with you.*

*Faith of Peace*

## DAY 38

*Do You Believe in Prayer?*

Of course I believe in prayer. All this time, I've longed to have someone to love, and through patience God brought Christión into my life. I'm not saying that I needed a man to complete my life, but when I became strong enough to move on by myself, the subtle power of faith led me to a committed relationship.

The man of my desire did not come in the package that I thought he would: I'm not saying that Christión is physically unattractive; he is very laid back. He does not dress up; I don't even think he owns a suit or a tie. He usually works behind the scenes, and he can fade away into the background if you're not looking, kind of like I used to do when I was younger. But through loyalty and prayer, his presence was drawn to me, and I toward him. Yes, I believe in prayer!

---

*God is our father in heaven, and we are his sons and daughters on earth. At times, it may not seem as if he listens—or even cares, for that matter—but he is the strength that surges through our body, holding us up when everything in life threatens to beat us down. Don't lose heart! Believe!*

*Faith of Peace*

*Define friendship.*
*Companionship, a closeness that conquers animosity*

## DAY 39

*Do You Care about Friendship?*

Yes, I believe in friendship. That's how Christión and I started out: as friends. Infatuation never played a part in our relationship in the beginning—at least not for me it didn't—but in the end, our friendship led us to become lovers, which eventually led to marriage!

---

*Good friendships are hard to come by, so when you embark upon a bond that is golden, cherish it—especially if this gift is found within your soul mate!*

*Faith of Peace*

# DAY 40

*Do You Like Where You Are in Life?*

It took a long while for me to accept where I was in life. My life was leading me; never once did I believe that I had the power to take control of my own journey. I was taught to work hard and pay my bills, and that if I was lucky, I could enjoy the extras that this world had to offer, such as materialistic values. Worldly desires got old real quick for me. I wanted a life that held value and purpose; I now longed for a good marriage and children. My life did not match up with the storybook romances that I would witness in the movies or on TV. I felt as if I was missing out on something that was meant to stabilize my future. I was a walking wreck, hoping that somehow I would end up where I needed to be by chance; yet, I was in spiritual pain. I came to realize that life was not meant to be lived in a routine manner. When I met Christión, I knew he was right for me; as our time progressed together, I knew he was the man that God had designed to fit into my life.

I was engulfed in the fast-paced world of modeling, ongoing appointments, and hotels, and was surrounded by the concrete jungle, pagers, cell phones, iPhones, all sorts of handheld devices —the list went on and on. And Christión was the complete opposite; he was surrounded by cedar, pine, lakes—and most important of all, peace. I'm happy to say that opposites do attract—in my case, that is. Eventually, I got out of the business, and Christión and I married. He found a position for me in his company; nothing big, just a title he made up for me. Basically, I take messages and return phone calls. I had to learn to speak up;

people often complained that I was hard to hear. I'd rather communicate by e-mail. I hate talking on the phone; just another one of my bashful crutches that I'll just have to get over, I guess. Yet, my best role ever is motherhood! We had a son; his name is Tristón.

I felt the need to give closure to the women who shared my pain; I know that there are women out there who are starting out on a journey of inner healing similar to my excursion in life; it is important that you all know that I survived my heartache! The key to recovery was letting go in faith, which has led me to grace.

Not only did I have to let go of my ex-husband, I also had to let go of the old Judie, and I did so without looking back. I'm not ashamed of that shy, hopeless woman; my brokenness at that time emerged into strength, transforming me into the woman, the wife, and the mother I am today. Through my pain, I'm able to educate my children so that they can live a purposeful life— and yes, I said children: I'm pregnant the second time around, and it's a girl! I was frightened to have a daughter, not wanting to pass on my bashful, hopeless curse, but that won't happen, because I have already endured her pain, so that she may have a full life that is built on the example of trust led by my husband and me. I'm no longer interested in resurfacing into this world as Judie the model. I hope to go into the medical field and work in the children's ward someday, in God's perfect timing. Yet, to every woman who struggles with letting go of their unfaithful husbands, I have this advice: If he is not willing to change through the power of commitment and faith, let him go. That unfaithful husband of yours is disturbing your peace!

Love,
Judie, a.k.a. Serenity! 😊

# Infidelity through Dreams

A famous Hollywood producer shared his weakness behind infidelity when his wife revealed their "million-dollar agreement" on ABC's talk show *The View*. The Mrs. informed her husband that he could cheat; however, he'd have to pay her a million dollars each time he did so.

"I didn't just call up my wife and say, 'Can I go sleep with somebody and give you a million dollars?'" the producer voiced. "I'm not foolish."

The first "affair" was with a woman who came on to the producer while he was at the office. He then took the woman to the mansion that he and his wife both shared. Needless to say, the security guards that were asked to keep watch slipped up. The wealthy producer had to give in, admitting that he had a woman at the house; due to his infidelity, a million-dollar agreement between this cheating man and his wife emerged. I don't understand the concept behind their agreement, but one thing is clear: the producer's wife is having a hard time letting go—but at a million dollars a cheat, perhaps he's worth holding on to, one might think. At least now she can hire a private investigator.

But what woman wants to stay up pondering if her husband is cheating or not? What about sexually transmitted diseases or a child born out of infidelity, all due to selfish and reckless behavior?

Infidelity is a plague that does not discriminate, and at some point we either know of someone who has been affected by this pestering curse, or we have suffered personally.

Men and women have reached out in search of why their spouses choose to cheat. Some say they suspect that their spouse may be having an affair, but they are not certain. Trust your instincts, which may even reveal the truth in dreams; odd but true.

There were many dream prophets in the Bible who interpreted poignant visions that helped to protect generations from famine and physical harm. Daniel and Joseph are among the two most popular dream spiritualists; each had gifts that they shared with others, giving credit to an all-knowing God.

Dreams of infidelity may be warning signs.

I once had a woman tell me that her ten-year-old daughter had a dream that her dad had taken off on a bicycle with another woman. This woman shared that her little girl's dream held truth; her husband was indeed having an affair. The only true way to understand if a suspicious dream has merit is to allow time to reveal the truth.

# Till Divorce Do Us Part

Many women mourn the loss of a perfect relationship through poetry.

And some women express the pain of what could have been through lyrics.

A young artist, wise before her time, Miss, Understood, shares her pain of divorce through the art of poetry.

## Till Divorce Do Us Part

What we said was till death do us part.
I opened my soul and gave u my heart.
On that day I became we, united, a team.
It was just u and me, together forever,
or so I thought.

But six months in was when u got caught!
It was a mistake; I love you, you said,
don't let other people get in your head,
nothing even happened; you are my life,
you have my kids, you are my wife.

You asked for forgiveness and so in I gave.
I chewed up the pain and swallowed the rage.
After all I have no real proof,
only a rumor and u being aloof.

I've seen this before but it can't be the same.
I mean he did change my last name.
So I let it go but it changed my perception,
it altered our bond and ruined our connection.

# God's Grace

There are poets such as Jonilynn, who rejoice in the hope that a perfect relationship has to offer.

*I feel so blessed, thankful, and amazed, to have everything I ever wanted because of God's grace.*

*The man of my dreams, without haze. For once my heart and mind are in the same place.*

*I feel butterflies throughout my body every time we kiss.*

*I've known him for years and finally can taste his lips. It's so real, raw, beautiful, and truly pure bliss.*

*I live every second in the moment, and cherish the sunlight glimpse.*

*Jonilynn*

# How Do I Forgive

Kim Corder, whom I called Ms. KC, lives in Arizona. Kim had built her experience on faithful knowledge, constructed on the most challenging familiarity of them all, that little thing called life. Kim's authentic testimony will resonate among many men and women, and hopefully her testimony will create an understanding behind the addiction of infidelity and the conclusion of reconciliation.

----

(Kim's Testimony)

As far back as I can remember, I've always known what I wanted to be when I grew up. More than anything else, I wanted to be a homemaker and mother. In high school, my greatest accomplishment was serving as president of the Future Homemakers of America. I was single-mindedly determined to do whatever it took to find, and marry, my Prince Charming, and then, live a white-picket-fence life.

# How Do I Forgive

My future Prince Charming and I met in the ninth grade, and we hit it off right away. We were best friends throughout high school, but we never dated until our senior year. He was outgoing, smart, and most important, funny.

It didn't matter what was going on at home, because I always knew when I got to school, he would make me laugh and feel better. Once we crossed that friend zone, it didn't take long for romance to blossom. We spent every single spare minute together that last year of high school and grew more in love every day.

A year after graduating high school, I married my best friend, and I truly thought, White-picket-fence life, here I come!

At first, married life was good. Not great, but good…at least for a few years. We'd argue about the typical things: sex and money. But since we didn't really have any money at the time, we mostly argued about sex. He wanted more, but I was too tired.

Things were far from ideal. Yet I tried to do my part. I enjoyed baking. That was my specialty: rich, creamy desserts made everything better for me and my family. The sinful sweets gave a false illusion that a certain hunger from within had been filled. Yet a sweet food addiction can be like any other addiction; once the fix is gone, it leaves you wanting more. This fixed illusion cannot compete with the harshness of reality.

And yet, I found myself clinging to my mother's marriage creed. She would say, "If he's not beating or cheating, then you shouldn't be bleating."

Mom religiously believed, practiced, and taught this dogma. It was her only criterion for a good marriage. She would often say, "What more could a woman ask for than a man who doesn't beat her or cheat on her?"

So I tried to convince myself that I was living the fairy-tale life. Yet for some reason, things just didn't feel very fairy-tale-ish.

Four years into the marriage, my so-called dream became a nightmare when my prince confessed to having an affair and wanted out of the marriage.

For some time, he had been telling me that he wasn't happy. He had even suggested seeing a marriage counselor, to which I responded, "Why? What we're going through are just normal growing pains in a young marriage."

In hindsight, all the warning signs were there, but…I just I chose to ignore them.

God knows the secrets of our hearts.

Many of you may not understand the living and all-knowing God. But as for me, having God in my life has become as crucial as the air to breathe.

On July 23, 2003, it was time for my husband's secret sexual sins to come into the light. God had decided that this was to be the day of reckoning. My husband had been caught, and his sex addiction could no longer be hidden. My heart was shattered, and I was completely devastated.

As I cried out to God, I began to experience a peace beyond understanding in the midst of this storm. I knew God was with me during this time, but I also knew He wasn't going to stop the pain or make the heartbreak go away. He gave constant reminders that He was right there with me as I experienced this excruciating pain. It felt like he was whispering in my ear, "I know this hurts, honey, but I'm right here."

John 16:33 assures us that "in this world you will have trouble." The harsh reality is that God rarely removes pain from our lives.

For many years, I thought that if I could just be a good Christian woman, God would reward me by giving me trials that were less painful. That is not true. God absolutely can give us peace in the midst of our pain, but rarely does He give peace in the place of our pain.

In my devastation and heartbreak, this verse was a lifesaver: "Do not be afraid; you will not be put to shame. Do not fear disgrace; you will not be humiliated. For your Maker is your husband—the Lord Almighty is his name. The Lord will call you back as if you were a wife deserted and distressed in spirit, a wife who married young, only to be rejected" (Isa. 54:4–6, NIV).

I felt these verses were written just for me. And I began to pursue God as my husband. My companion. My soul mate. He is trustworthy and faithful. He will never abandon me or betray me. He is the lover of my soul. His love is unconditional, unshakable, and true. This is what I've been longing for. This was true love!

Yet at the same time, I couldn't reason how to possibly make my broken, earthly marriage work to my broken, earthly husband. I couldn't get past feeling like I didn't deserve this. This wasn't fair. I felt there was no other choice but to divorce.

Then came the hardest part: telling the kids. Imagining their innocent hearts being crushed by this news was more than I could bear. I just couldn't do this to them. At that moment, I felt compelled to do whatever I could to try and save the marriage and our family, if for no other reason than for them.

I began to focus on how God could use our circumstances to help others. To see a greater purpose in all this mess gave me hope. Looking back now, I realize that what I really wanted was to rush the healing part of this process so that I could get to the helping-others part.

As God would have it, this type of healing cannot be rushed. I wanted God to quickly fix my husband and heal my hurts so that we could get on with our lives. Healing took much longer than I expected, and as I waited for it, I became more frustrated. After years of waiting, my frustration began to turn into anger, and that undealt-with anger eventually became full-on bitterness.

Anger and bitterness slammed hard into my heart. Boy, was I mad! I was mad at my circumstances, mad at my husband, and extremely angry at God. How could God let this happen? Bitterness became my addiction. I couldn't get rid of it. I would will myself to let go of the hurts and just choose to forgive, and it would work for a day or two or sometimes a week. Inevitably, something would trigger me and catapult me right back to the pit of bitterness.

I became suspicious about everything my husband was doing: every phone call, every lunch meeting, every business trip, everything. Soon my suspicion became obsession, and I was determined to catch him acting out in his sexual addiction. I spent hours snooping, looking for any shred of evidence that would convict him of wrongdoing. I peppered him daily with accusations. I condemned him and verbally and emotionally abused him on a daily basis. My distrust grew into disdain and eventually full-on disgust. I hated him and what he had done to our family. The more my bitterness took root, the more I gave in to it. Soon it had complete control over me.

Interestingly enough, during those years in bitterness, I was diligently spending time in Bible study. In the five years I spent spiraling out of control, I also completed more than ten Beth Moore Bible studies as well as a Celebrate Recovery step study. I was actively volunteering in ministry and spent more time pursuing God and in prayer than at any other time in my life— all the while steeped in anger, resentment, and bitterness.

I knew it was wrong and a sin to not forgive, yet I wasn't willing to let go of the hurt and forgive. Bitterness gave me a sense of control and strength that I had never experienced before. I liked the new me that didn't put up with getting taken advantage of.

Eventually, we sought out yet another marriage counselor, hoping this time it would help. We saw her twice a week for almost a year, but every time she would bring up what I call the dreaded "F" word—*forgive*—I would immediately shut down. Things were fine as long as we focused on my husband's need to change. I refused to address or even acknowledge that I had my own issues to work on.

I clearly remember the day she asked to meet with me alone. I entered her office expecting her to say that in her professional opinion, it would probably be best for Jim and me to just go ahead and separate.

Instead, she told me something that rocked my world that day. She said that she believed that if I were to die that day, that I—not my husband—would be the one held accountable for the unhealthy state of my marriage.

She went on to explain that since I was the one refusing to change, forgive, and trust God, that I was also the one now doing damage to the marriage. It was no longer my husband's behaviors that were hurting us, but instead my bitterness was barreling us toward divorce. I felt as though she had just sucker punched me right in the gut. I left her office stunned, confused, and hopeless.

I was overwhelmed by the weight of it all. This all seemed so unfair! I didn't betray the marriage. How could I be responsible for it being broken now? This didn't make any sense to me. I was plagued with feelings that this wasn't right or fair, and I didn't deserve this! How can any of the blame of this struggling marriage be placed on me?

Yet I could clearly see the damage my bitterness was doing to my marriage. I looked at the way I was treating my husband as his just deserts, and I convinced myself that he deserved to be treated like a piece of dirt.

I spent hours flat on my face, crying out to God. I was desperate for something from Him. I begged Him to give me anything to help me figure out how to finally let go of my hurts, forgive my husband, and be free from this bitterness.

It was at this moment in my life in sheer desperation that God spoke to me, and I opened my Bible right to Psalm 55. Here, King David speaks of how a close friend's betrayal cuts deeply. He says that he can endure it when an enemy betrays him, but when it's a close friend or companion that has broken his promises, this type of betrayal causes him great distress.

As I'm reading this psalm, I get to verse twenty-two, and I know in my heart that this is the answer to my desperate plea to figure out how to forgive. There, David tells me exactly what I need to do with my all my disappointment, resentment, unforgiveness, and bitterness. It's simple yet profound: "Cast your cares on the Lord and He will sustain you."

As soon as I read that verse, I knew it was my answer, my solution, and my salvation from bitterness. God was instructing me to give Him all my cares. This includes my hurts, concerns, worries, fears, sadness, anger, and distrust.

As I continued to read that psalm, I knew I had found my mecca. The very last sentence says it all: "But as for me, I trust in you."

I knew in my heart that I had just been handed the keys to unlocking this prison of bitterness. At that moment, I wrote these words in the margin next to that psalm: *Today has been one of the hardest days so far! God brought me to this Psalm. Lord, help me to trust in you. May this be a turning point in my ability to let go and finally forgive.*

Praise God, that was the turning point! I started letting go of my hurts and trusting God with the rest. The mess that took me years to create but only took God a month to the day to fix. Thirty days later, I revisited Psalm 55 and penned the words, *Today I am grateful that God is faithful. I think I've finally figured out how to forgive.*

Since then, God has given me a brand-new heart toward my husband. I am so grateful to say that not only do I love my husband, but I actually like him as a person, and that's huge for me! Not only that, but I truly enjoy spending time with him. More than anything, I look forward to growing old with him.

Figuring out how to forgive was something that I did the hard way. I tried everything else besides forgiving, and none of it worked for me.

Today there are two things I can say with complete confidence regarding forgiveness:

Number one, forgiveness isn't easy or simple. For me, it's been the single most challenging thing I have ever done.

Number two, forgiveness is worth it. Forgiveness doesn't make what was done to you okay. It will never be okay God has shown me that you don't forgive for the person who hurt or betrayed you; it's for you. Forgiveness is what's best for you.

The serenity prayer says, "Trusting that you will make all things right if I surrender to your will."

In my life, there has been a direct correlation between surrendering to God's will and things being made right in my life.

# How Do I Forgive

This journey has taught me how to really trust in the Lord. I know now what it means to surrender my life to God's will. I am grateful for the lessons I've learned because they are why I'm where I am today. One thing I know, regardless what the future holds, I will never struggle with unforgiveness or bitterness at the same level that I once did.

There was a time when my life was out of control. Full of doubts that have plagued my being since I was child. Always hoping and wishing that someone would be able to see inside my fragile heart. I was way too trusting in the past, allowing man to steer my heart in the right direction. Not understanding that men were just as lost and vulnerable as women. The difference is that the defenselessness of man drives the need for understanding into a dark pit covered with guilt and shame. How could I expect someone who masked his feelings to validate me as person? How could I expect a man deepened in his own insecurities to secure my doubts and fears as a wife and a mother?

Only through the trials of deep-rooted pain was I able to dwell in my weakness, groaning through the agony of time in search for a cause which would define me as something other than a deceived wife and a disappointed mother.

I've now been married for more than thirty years. Time had a way of uncovering a strength based on trials and tribulations. No one has faith of steel. We all have our weakness, and mine was fear embedded in mistrust. I relied on the wrong concepts of life to keep me safe. I was disappointed time and time again. Building a relationship within myself that forced me to rely on a connection that was beyond human control was my release. This relationship belonged to me alone, and no man—not even my husband—could perceive the glorious foundation of trust that I now depended on.

Through this newfound affiliation, I could not fault my husband for his inadequacies without discerning my own nature and motives in life. I could not hold my God-given mate up to the standards of perfection when the same proficiencies did not exist in me. I took ownership of validating the only being that could authenticate me. That presence survives through the spirit that had shaped itself inside of me since birth. Through understanding, I now speak to the lowly woman who looks toward earthly values and man to fulfill her void or to define her value in this dark and very complex world.

I praise the temperament that awakened my self-worth. My new gift in life is to stir that safe spirit of comfort in all women, having faith that all women will have the courage to receive it.

*(Author Kim Corder)*

# The Ultimate Marriage

I had a dream in which I was overlooking a striking vision of a beautiful woman in great bodily form, reminiscent of an Olympic athlete.

Her arms were chiseled, her legs were strong and well defined.

Her visible motion consisted of running in a gliding motion, back and forth, along a narrow, repetitious path.

With determination and vigor similar to that of a seasoned athlete, the expression on her face revealed that there was a deeper passion.

Her eyes were intensely shut, as if she had been on this journey for a long time.

I could that tell her determination was securely embedded deep within her heart!

While the athlete was meditating on the race before her, a compelling, deep chime of rhythmic music submerged in power filled the space.

# The Ultimate Marriage

A man of the same physical beauty as the woman descended from heaven, and they embraced in a whirlwind of vibrant color.

His presence swept around the woman, and his body without hesitation merged with hers.

The two were now united into one being, and as the colorful current swept away this newly formed image, they embraced in the thunder of music, disappearing like mist into the depths of heaven.

This transformation left behind a vivid essence of color similar to that of a rainbow, leading me to believe that through perseverance, there is a different kind of marriage that exists between humans and our creator.

A good friend and talented artist, Ms. Abril, describes the perfect marriage through her love for art:

> When I'm designing furniture, I'm excited about the texture and the nature of the wood. Each piece has a unique quality.
> I don't try to design all of my pieces the same because that takes away from the wood's natural form. Relationships are the same way.
> You have to allow a person to be who they are and learn from their own mistakes to develop genuine values within themselves.

Abril is right. How many times have we tried to fix our partner to fit into our mold? Women desperately crave the perfect relationships—we honestly try to help—yet we don't want to be the kind of woman who constantly tries to control our mate out of fear.

Through experience, a wise source, a woman known as May, shared that you can't change a person; they have to be willing to make a difference on their own terms. Women must lean of faith through patience, believing that change is possible and that their mate is worth saving.

For those who believe, we strive to do the things in life that please a forgiving and patient God, the Alpha and the Omega. Like the athlete in the dream, we won't always do exactly what God expects, but the key point is that we are striving, racing back and forth in life in an effort to make things right. When our trial is complete, the results will please our heavenly father, and in return, he will embrace his children, sending down a blessing of acceptance, graduating his children onto eternal life.

To those looking for change, what should you do? Find a great Bible-based church, not a church that is looking to control your mind. Search for the church that is spiritually prepared to grow you and set you free in Christ!

Yes, there are some bad churches out there! But there are some good ones, too. Finding a church is like shopping for a car or a mate! There are some liars and lemons out there, but this does not mean that you stop searching for a car or mate in fear of a possible liar or lemon. In all you do, keep searching until you find the ride that best suits your journey.

Start off with a home-based Bible study if you have to. And avoid routine religion! God does not want a robot! He wants you and all of your baggage. Trust me. He is more than qualified to handle it.

There will be bumps along the way, but it's totally worth it in the end. And trust me, the road does end eventually—enjoy the ride!

*Faith of peace be with you!*
*Emunah La-Paz*

1.800.799.SAFE (7233) 1.800.787.3224
Anonymous & Confidential Help 24/7
Credit
Kim Corder, author of the upcoming book
*The Scent of Lavender: Finding Peace in Letting Go*
Jonilynn
Foreword Irene Roth

# About the Author

Emunah La-Paz writes about real-life issues that are based on actual events. Emunah's mission is to bring awareness to hidden addictions and social issues that hinder divine awareness and bring women together in hopes of encouraging one another to discover the hope and courage to live a healthier and productive life.

Emunah dedicates her time to volunteering for various causes that help support women and children in Arizona.

*Photograph by Nancy Hall*

---

Look out for the documentary inspired by this book.

*Born Sexy Yesterday*:
*Decoding the Enigma of Eternal Beauty*

Visit the author's website at www.emunahlapaz.com

www.ingramcontent.com/pod-product-compliance
Lightning Source LLC
Chambersburg PA
CBHW062050270326
41931CB00013B/3014